GREAT FRENCH CHEFS

and their recipes

Editor
Céline Martin-Raget

Art Director
Antoine de Payrat

Design
Isabelle Ducat and Anne-Lou Bissières

Translated from the French by
Louise Guiney

Copyediting
Penny Isaac

Proofreading
Susan Schneider and Kimberly Conniff Taber

Color Separation
Dupont Photogravure

Simultaneously published in French as
France Des Chefs © Éditions Flammarion,
2003. English-language edition
© Éditions Flammarion, 2003
26, rue Racine
75006, Paris

03 04 05 4 3 2 1

FA1170-03-IX
ISBN: 2-0801-1170-1
Dépôt légal: 09/2003

Printed in Italy by Rotolito Lombarda

Conversions		
Flour 1 cup	125g	4 oz
Sugar 1 cup	250g	8 oz
Heavy cream 1 cup	250g	8 oz
Rice (uncooked) 1 cup	220g	7 oz
Liquids ¼ cup	60 ml	2 fl oz
⅓ cup	80 ml	2 ¾ fl oz
½ cup	125 ml	4 fl oz
¾ cup	185 ml	6 fl oz
1 cup	250 ml	8 fl oz

TEXT BY JEAN-LOUIS ANDRÉ
PHOTOGRAPHY BY JEAN-FRANÇOIS MALLET

GREAT FRENCH CHEFS

and their recipes

Flammarion

CONTENTS

INTRODUCTION

They're masters of the culinary arts, and also men who know how to manage a team, a dining room, a business. They create recipes; they command their troops. They're artists and businessmen, stage directors and chief executives, one-man bands and orchestral conductors. They're rewarded with stars that sometimes fall, or that sometimes remain fixed in the sky above them. They often serve as France's cultural ambassadors to the rest of the world. They have imitators, and they have acolytes. There are cooks outside of France, to be sure—many of them extremely talented. But inside France, chefs are monarchs. They reign supreme.

There was once a time when even the most brilliant chefs remained anonymous. They were employees. In those days, people boasted of dining at Maxim's or the Tour d'Argent. Today people boast of dining with Billon, Passard, or Meneau. Chefs are no longer confined to the obscurity of their pantries. These sons of Bocuse (who was the first to pose for the magazine *Paris Match*, when he won his third Michelin star in 1965) have now joined architects and grand couturiers in the media's artistic pantheon. It matters little that chefs work to order in an ephemeral medium. They create. That is, they amaze us, fuel our dreams, erase the borders between continents. They improvise; they have signature dishes. Like composers or painters, they compellingly project their own personalities.

The question is not whether they're physically present in their restaurants, whether they carry out the crucial gestures themselves or delegate the work to an assistant—son, wife, kindred spirit, team. Some rarely set foot in their kitchens; others never miss a meal. Who can say which is right? Absentee chefs regard their kitchens as studios, in the sense understood by Renaissance sculptors; whereas others, heirs to the romantic tradition, believe in the solitary inspiration of the artist. The main thing, when all is said and done, is the incredible creative energy possessed by all of them.

Marc Haeberlin, Anne-Sophie Pic, Gérard Boyer, Gérald Passédat, and many like them are outstanding representatives of this evolution. The offspring of culinary

dynasties, they learned their craft at their parents' knees. They grew up among sauce bases, beurre blanc, and the carefully choreographed ballet of servers. But, in order to progress, they had to venture off the beaten path. They had to plumb their own psyches to find out what they wanted to say and how to say it. Following in a father's footsteps is a good way to start out in the culinary field, but it's not enough. Major battles still lie ahead. Fine cuisine isn't just a matter of expertise. It requires a taste for risk.

Listen to Marc Haeberlin as he contemplates the path he has traveled, speaking from his inn where the river, running below, exudes a timeless air. As he tells it, the time is long gone when chefs could earn three Michelin stars with traditional dishes such as sole *dieppoise*. Over the past twenty years, as chefs began to appear on television screens and were written up in popular magazines, consumer demands and attitudes changed. People now want light food, exotic combinations, short cuts between cultures, ellipses. Fine cuisine has followed in the wake of contemporary art.

And yet, history and tradition have not been completely cast aside. Even an avant-gardist such as Alain Passard earned his stripes catering weddings and banquets. Self-taught chefs—the ones who took up the craft in response to a passion, an instinct—have nevertheless all followed at least a part of the path traced by their elders. And even the erstwhile student of chemistry, Olivier Roellinger, took time out for a brief but useful tour of duty with established leaders in the field before branching out to create his own highly personal cuisine. The desire to be an artist is one thing; actually becoming one is something else. The lessons of the past are no less valuable when it comes to pioneering a sweet-and-sour sauce.

In cuisine, as elsewhere, conflicts will inevitably arise between the old school and the new: traditional sauces versus pan juices, emulsions versus syrups, mousses versus creams,

olive oil versus butter. Ranged on one side of the battlefield are the lovers of regional produce, old-fashioned markets, and the French home cooking on which that country's culinary reputation has rested ever since the days of Escoffier. These are the people who favor long-simmering and classic recipes, the people who respect a perfect soufflé. On the opposite end stand those who want to investigate different cultures. Those who recognize that French cuisine was at its most brilliant in the seventeenth century, when it welcomed the beans, potatoes, tomatoes, and other hybrids imported from the Americas. This modern camp points out that today distances are telescoped, that it takes more time to procure carrots from Mont Saint Michel than truffles from Italy. Contemporary cuisine has speeded up. It can now embrace both summer and winter, Europe and Asia, cherries and Szechuan pepper. Of course, there are also contemporary chefs who decide to return to the fold. One of them is Alain Passard, who has literally gone back to his roots, basing his cuisine on the fine produce from his own vegetable garden.

We wanted to meet some of these artists. Not just to study their recipes, but to really get to know them. Our first question addressed their personal experience, our second the genesis of their vocation. Then we tried to understand how, in relation to a native land either drawn upon or rejected, they constructed their individual spiritual landscapes. And, lastly, we attempted to describe their creative processes. The book that emerged from these meetings is certainly not exhaustive. Its choices are arbitrary—choices conditioned by the goal of illustrating, as vividly as possible, a diversity of regional influences and the immense variety found under the single title, "chef." We met a gamut of individuals ranging from the virtuoso to the eloquent, the media star to the commercial powerhouse, the taciturn to the voluble, the anguished to the self-assured. Today's chefs represent a touch of France.

GEORGES BILLON

GRAND HÔTEL DE CALA ROSSA

CORSICA

THE MAN

Two skippers man the helm at the Grand Hôtel de Cala Rossa. Georges Billon is the one dressed in white. He has been at his post for some twenty years past and claims he feels so at home here, he's never been tempted to open his own restaurant. He also points out that what goes on in his kitchen fits into a strategy formulated by the other skipper, the Boss.

The Boss, Toussaint Canarelli, immediately returns the compliment. Neither professional chef nor hotelier himself, this erstwhile butcher/*charcutier*/horse-trader has an unfailing instinct about hiring the right people. His hotel—a major Corsican institution with a staff of some one hundred people—would be nothing without Georges Billon. "Look at those rooms we haven't gotten around to decorating yet. Our reputation obviously doesn't have anything to do with our rooms, and everything to do with our cuisine. When it comes to cuisine, Georges is in charge."

Georges Billon moved to Corsica because he couldn't live anywhere else. After sixteen years in Morocco and a stint in Savoy, he tried Lyon, where his family now lives. But Lyon was too gloomy for him; too depressing, after sixteen years of Moroccan sunshine. "In Corsica, I was looking for the sunny south." Toussaint Canarelli's newly acquired Cala Rossa was the perfect answer. This hotel, crying out for imaginative restoration, stands at the southern tip of the sunny south, on the gulf of Porto-Vecchio.

It was as a teenager in Morocco that Georges first developed an interest in cuisine. He came by it honestly. "My parents ran the laundry in a large hotel. I grew up watching them iron white coats and starch chefs' hats." The family's attitudes did the rest. "My father was a terrific gourmet. He spent all his free time copying recipes into a big notebook, and every once in a while he'd try one."

Georges went on to train in some of France's foremost restaurants, an apprenticeship following old-school methods. "Skilled craftsmen taught me their principles and

their philosophy. Always go beyond the strict minimum. Master the basics before launching into flamboyant showpieces. Think of each dish as a modest construction built on a raw product." Georges has never experienced the thrill—or the stress—of three-star status. One star is enough for him. "This way, I have a free hand." Free, in other words, to invent his own semi-sophisticated cuisine, which is still a rarity on an island where "gastronomy" refers to plain home cooking rather than to the delicacies in luxury restaurants.

THE REGION

Georges Billon isn't Corsican by birth, but after twenty years working on the island he's become Corsican by adoption. For example, he never misses the Bocognano Chestnut Festival, which displays the very best chestnut flours available and provides an introduction to a venerable tradition. Georges has also visited dozens of cheese- and sausage-makers in remote mountain areas. He has sampled, asked questions, discussed, learned. He's often impressed, and just as often disappointed. "When I started out, I discovered that any given supplier could nosedive from the top of the heap to the bottom. Also, the rapid expansion of the tourist trade has undermined the old standards."

Today Georges Billon is sure of himself. First, because he knows exactly where to go to get precisely what he wants. He's made friends with three fishermen in Porto-Vecchio who'll cast their nets for him and bring in a couple dozen red mullet. He buys from the two master *charcutiers*—one in the Ajaccio area, the other near Levie in Alta Rocca—who consistently produce the best ham. He knows a shepherd near the hotel whose cheese is unique because his sheep graze on open meadows. He is also sure of himself because Corsica itself is changing, returning to its roots. Georges goes to the Anghione Plateau in the Antisanti Mountains for an olive oil with a bitter-almond after-taste that's as smooth as velvet. This oil, from groves on the Marquiliani estate, is a

Page 12:
Olives from the
Marquiliani estate.

Page 13:
Georges Billon with
Anne Amalric of the
Marquiliani estate.

Left to right:
Coppa is best
when sliced thin.
Honey from the slopes
of the Bavella.
Sheep's cheese produced
by shepherd Antoine Foata,
who is also a neighbor.

*The wild coastline
of southern Corsica.*

three-time winner of gold medals in numerous international competitions. Honey and
brocciù cheese reflect the same renewed quest for authenticity. "You can tell a good
brocciù immediately. It's not watery; you can use it without draining."

In Corsica, as elsewhere, you have to respect the seasons. Serve figatelli (Corsican
giblet sausage) on cold winter evenings, stuff eggplant with basil rather than brocciù
in summer, since that's when all the goats' milk goes to the newborn kids. Although
Georges's repertoire includes several popular local dishes, such as pasta with crayfish,
roast capon, or veal with olives, he bears in mind that he's not a true native and never
embarks on Corsican "soul food." "Bean soup and chestnut-flour *pulenda* are served
at excellent mountain inns. I don't want to trespass on that terrain. Some purist would
inevitably point out exactly where I'd gone wrong."

THE STYLE

First, take a look at the terrace. It's vast, dotted with pine trees that afford glimpses of
the beach beyond. Informally dressed diners drop in between swims. Is this really the
kind of place for haute cuisine? Is gourmet dining compatible with the carefree holiday spirit? Yes, if the chef is willing to work a little differently.

Willing, first of all, to feed the multitudes, which can mean crowds of around 150
at the season's peak. This rules out elaborate preparations. "I keep things simple, and
not just for practical reasons I also do it because I know my guests aren't interested in
over-sophisticated cuisine. They can get that back home." Most of his guests are
Parisians taking a break from their usual routine. Here they're looking for something

good, but not too heavy. Tasty but not complicated. Roast milk-fed lamb with herbs, baked rockfish or denti (a large local species), and roast duckling with honey are all fine, provided they're perfectly cooked. "I've stopped using butter and cream. My preference is for a cuisine of subtle fragrances." The challenge is to do it perfectly. Under these conditions, if this kind of chef wants to keep his Michelin star, he has to work faultlessly.

Although the Cala Rossa's guests may appreciate a light hand behind the stove, they still want to be impressed when they sit down each night. Most people stay at the hotel for a week or two and eat at least one meal per day there. They don't want a big production number, but they do want dishes that are both familiar and intriguing. "Over a span of at least two weeks, I have to offer a range of different choices each night, and this forces me to improvise on the basis of what's available at the market. I'm always experimenting." Georges's experiments include scrambled eggs with sea urchin and chestnut-flour pound cake. "Every morning I face the same challenge: motivating the hotel's guests to gather later on my terrace after a day at the beach. I want them to anticipate that moment throughout their entire day."

Facing page:
The cliffs of Bonifacio.

Right:
Catching rock fish.

Far right:
Olive oil with a taste of the wild.

SERVES 4
For the fennel aspic
- 3 sheets gelatin
- ¼ fennel bulb
- 1 teaspoon olive oil
- ½ teaspoon anisette
- 1 cup water
- Salt, pepper

For the sea urchins
- 16 sea urchins
- 2 sheets gelatin
- Juice of 1 lemon
- ½ cup hazelnut oil
- Salt, pepper

PREPARATION TIME
45 minutes

COOKING TIME
30 minutes

*Temporary beachfront restaurants:
a seasonal tradition in this resort.*

Corsican Sea Urchins with Fennel Aspic

• *Preparing the fennel aspic*: Soak the 3 sheets of gelatin in a little cold water. Rinse and coarsely chop the fennel. Heat the olive oil in a small saucepan, add the chopped fennel and the anisette. Simmer, stirring constantly, for 10 minutes, or until translucent. Season to taste. Add the water and simmer gently for 30 minutes without stirring. Strain this liquid into a bowl. Add the softened gelatin and whip until dissolved. Season to taste and set aside at room temperature.

• *Preparing the sea urchins*: Soak the 2 sheets of gelatin in a little cold water. Using a small pair of scissors, open the sea urchins. Drain the juices into a bowl and gently remove the meat with a teaspoon. Set the 24 shapeliest pieces of meat aside on a plate.

Strain the sea-urchin juices and combine them with the remaining sea-urchin meat in a small pot. Heat this mixture for 1 minute without boiling, add the softened gelatin and lemon juice. Season to taste and whip until the gelatin is dissolved and all the ingredients are thoroughly blended. Cool and then mix in blender with the hazelnut oil.

Wash the sea-urchin shells under a stream of cold water. Fill the clean shells with the hazelnut-oil preparation. Allow to gel for 10 minutes in the refrigerator. Garnish each shell with one of the pieces of sea-urchin meat previously set aside. Cover with 2 tablespoons of the fennel aspic and allow to gel for 20 minutes in the refrigerator.

Red Mullet Stuffed with Brocciù

SERVES 4
- 4 whole red mullet, boned (ask your fish vendor to do this)
- ½ lb Swiss chard, green leafy part only
- 1 lb brocciù (creamy white Corsican cheese)
- 1 egg yolk
- 1 teaspoon pine nuts, grilled and chopped
- 1 teaspoon chopped mixed dried herbs
- ½ cup olive oil
- Salt, pepper

PREPARATION TIME
35 minutes

COOKING TIME
25 minutes

Preheat the oven to 350°F (180°C).

Cook the chard in boiling salted water. Drain and chop.

In a bowl, mix together the brocciù, egg yolk, chopped chard, pine nuts, herbs, and 5 tablespoons of the olive oil. Season to taste and stuff the red mullet with this mixture.

Place the stuffed fish in a large earthenware baking dish. Season with salt and pepper, and cover with the remaining olive oil. (The fish can also be individually wrapped and tied in a large vine leaf to prevent the stuffing from spilling out during cooking.)

Bake the fish for 25 minutes.

Serve whole, accompanied by a salad.

Spaghetti with Rock Lobster

SERVES 4
- 2 small rock lobsters weighing 3 lb each, or 1 large rock lobster weighing 5 lb or more
- 8 oz spaghetti
- 3 cloves garlic
- 10 tablespoons olive oil
- 1 bouquet garni
- 1 cup fish stock
- 1 teaspoon tomato paste
- 1 cup white wine
- ½ bunch basil
- Salt, pepper

PREPARATION TIME
45 minutes

COOKING TIME
40 minutes

Cook the spaghetti in a large pot of boiling salted water until it is al dente. Drain, rinse, and set aside at room temperature.

Cook the rock lobster(s) for 2 minutes in a large pot of boiling water. Drain. Remove the meat from the tails in a single piece. Use a teaspoon to scrape the coral and creamy matter out of the heads. Coarsely chop the shells from the heads. Place the shells in a bowl and set aside in the refrigerator.

Peel and chop the garlic cloves.

Heat 4 tablespoons olive oil in a frying pan and sauté the medallions of tail meat for 1 minute on each side. Drain and set aside on a plate.

In the same pan, lightly sauté the shells with the bouquet garni. Add 1 cup water or fish stock and reduce over low heat to three-quarters of the original volume. Strain this broth into a bowl. Heat 4 tablespoons olive oil in a flameproof casserole, add the chopped garlic, stir for 1 minute, add the tomato paste. Stir and add 1 cup white wine. Simmer this sauce for 3 minutes over a low heat, then add the stock made from the shells. Simmer for 5 minutes to reduce again somewhat, add the lobster coral, whip lightly, remove from heat, and season to taste.

Add the cooked spaghetti, the remaining olive oil, and the lobster medallions to the casserole. Sprinkle with chopped basil leaves and reheat. Serve very hot.

SERVES 4
- 4 partridges
- Olive oil
- 1 clove garlic
- ½ cup clear myrtle spirits (or brandy)
- 4 long thin slices bacon
- ½ cup white wine
- 2 sprigs fresh myrtle
- 1 bouquet garni
- ½ cup chicken stock
- Salt, pepper

For the stuffing
- 5 oz cèpes
- 4 oz chanterelles
- 2 oz craterellus mushrooms
- 1½ oz sausage meat
- 1½ oz Corsican figatelli sausage
- 3 oz chestnuts, chopped

For the Chestnut polenta
- 2 cups heavy cream
- 1 cup chestnut flour
- Dash of ground nutmeg

PREPARATION TIME
45 minutes

COOKING TIME
40 minutes

Roast Stuffed Partridge and Myrtle with Chestnut Polenta

• *Preparing the stuffing*: Wash and chop the mushrooms, sauté in olive oil, and mix with the sausage meat, figatelli, and chestnuts.

• *Preparing the partridges*: Preheat oven to 325°F (160°C). Season the partridges with salt and pepper. Heat some olive oil in a cast-iron casserole, add the garlic, and brown the partridges on all sides in the oil. Add the clear myrtle spirits and flame. Remove from heat.

Drain the browned partridges on a large plate, fill them with the mushroom stuffing, and wrap a slice of bacon around each one. Place the partridges in an earthenware baking dish and roast for 30 minutes.

Meanwhile reheat the casserole, deglaze with white wine, add the sprigs of myrtle and bouquet garni. Reduce the liquid in the casserole by one-half, add the chicken stock. Season to taste and simmer for 10 minutes, stirring occasionally. When the sauce is smooth and thickened, strain and keep warm.

• *Preparing the chestnut polenta*: Scald 2 cups heavy cream and whisk in the chestnut flour. Season to taste with salt, pepper, and a dash of nutmeg. Continue stirring until thickened and smooth. Add 2 tablespoons olive oil.

Remove the partridges from the oven, arrange on a large platter. Add the juices from the baking dish to the sauce and serve separately with the chestnut polenta.

Awaiting the crowd.

SERVES 4
- 5 oz chestnut paste
- 6 tablespoons softened butter and butter for greasing
  the molds
- 3 eggs & 3 egg yolks
- 2 tablespoons sugar
- 1½ tablespoons flour &
  1½ tablespoons chestnut
  flour
- ½ teaspoon baking powder

PREPARATION TIME
30 minutes

COOKING TIME
10 minutes

Sampling olive oil.

Tender Chestnut Cake

In a large bowl, whip together the chestnut purée with the softened butter and the whole eggs.

Beat the egg yolks in another bowl, add the sugar, and continue beating for 10 minutes until the mixture is smooth and pale yellow.

Beat the flour and baking powder into the contents of the second bowl, and then fold the contents of one bowl into the contents of the other.

Butter 4 ramekins (approximately 2 inches [5-6 cm] high) and chill for 2 minutes in the refrigerator.

Preheat oven to 350°F (180°C).

Ten minutes before serving, pour the dough into the ramekins, filling about halfway. Bake for exactly 10 minutes. Remove from oven and allow to rest for 2 minutes before serving. The interior of the cakes should be very soft.

PAUL BOCUSE

L'AUBERGE DE COLLONGES

COLLONGES

THE MAN

Some of the best houses in Lyon have a portrait of Monsieur Paul on the wall. This legendary figure strikes his pose on the premises of Colette Sibilla, queen of the pistachio cervelat sausage, the rosette salami, and the no-nonsense blue apron. He reigns over the home of La Mère Richard, a childhood friend in whose cellars Saint Marcellin cheese slowly loses its Isère identity and becomes totally Lyonnais. The man wearing the red, white, and blue collar of a humble "Meilleur Ouvrier de France" and a chef's hat as imposing as the Eiffel Tower, his arms akimbo, is clearly not camera-shy. He readily admits to assuming a role when he enters his dining room; he seems to take on the strength of an icon. He's the living hero of his own frescoes—one outside L'Auberge de Collonges, the other in town on the banks of the Saône.

Seeing him in the flesh is another matter. These portraits are like the images of France's president hanging in town halls: their subject is actually far away. On a plane to Orlando, for example, since he's opened a restaurant for Disney. Or in the process of preparing the Bocuse d'Or awards—an annual event honoring some of the world's chefs, and an astute way of placing himself a notch above them. Or he might be checking on the renovations at his latest brasserie. His current strategy is to center Lyon in relation to the cardinal points of the compass. First there was Le Nord, then Le Sud. L'Est, a huge techno-Californian establishment, occupies the old Les Brotteaux railroad station. L'Ouest is almost finished, and will serve 800 meals daily.

Some mornings you might find Bocuse taking time off for a coffee in his friend Vavro's kitchen. A native of Lyon with Slavic roots, illustrator and designer Vavro is the man responsible for honing the Bocuse image. He's the one who dreamed up the casual décor of Bocuse's new brasseries, where he didn't stint on color. The servers wear earphones and mikes, and orders are placed on computers. Modern. By contrast, the atmosphere of the main restaurant, the one in Collonges, has been left unchanged.

This is the site of L'Auberge, the inn run by Bocuse's parents, where he was born in an upstairs room. Here, candelabra and fine silverware gleam on spotless white napery, the valet is dressed like a valet and not like a fashion model, the brass is polished daily by a brigade of busboys. Here, time has stood still. The tranquil France of old lives on.

If he can spare a moment, Monsieur Paul will show you his extraordinary collection of organs and barrel organs. He will pull out the stops himself, entranced with the music. He loves to hear the sound of old country-fair refrains ringing out just a step away from the riverside cafés along the Saône, in a manor house used for weddings and banquets that once belonged to his family—a house he swore he'd acquire himself, once he'd made his fortune. And there you have it. The strength of Bocuse—who is recognized, at the age of 75, as France's leading chef—resides in his ability to combine the iron will of a patriarch firmly attached to his roots, with the flair of a marketing expert. In Bocuse, improbably, Gnafron and Disney meet.

THE REGION

Before it evolved into an upper-class Lyon suburb, Collonges-aux-Monts-d'Or was a country village with its church, town hall, open market, winding alleyways and—below it—the Saône. Although there was no road from L'Auberge to the beach in those days, the gravel beach existed. There were bargemen, there were little riverside cafés, there were hunters who'd bring in a partridge or a brace of thrush. There were fishermen, tramps, and pretty young girls out for a stroll. In this world, people traveled by boat, bicycle, or—the lucky ones—in little Citroën "Deux Chevaux" cars. This was a world of family outings and Sunday picnics that might have come straight from a Renoir painting. This was the world Bocuse grew up in, and its contours live on in his imagination.

He's come a long way since then. But Collonges has always been the epicenter of the ever-widening circles in which he moves, a microcosm of the France he loves. He stands on tiptoe as his eyes rest on Lyon, a city where the enjoyment of fine food is as natural as breathing. From this vantage point, he can see the slopes where Charolais cattle graze. He can visualize, beyond, the sheep of the Auvergne and the Loire, Bresse chickens with their blue feet, the carp of Les Dombes, crayfish swimming in the streams of the Haute-Loire, the vineyards of Beaujolais and Côtes du Rhône. On a clear day, he can even visualize the blue cheeses of the Jura and the oysters of Cancale. Why not? They're all part of the gourmet picture. This is the mind that has made Bocuse an apostle of France's culinary treasures.

He knows how to pick and choose, and he's loyal to his friends—some would say his "gang." Long before everyone else began to go regional, Bocuse was the first to give credit to his suppliers, who are often listed on his menu. This is how the Lyon

confectioner Bernachon became one of the most famous chocolatiers in France, and this is how La Mère Richard grew prosperous in the marketplace. This is why Duboeuf, loaded down with fine wines, accompanies Bocuse on his world tours. Is that all there is to it? No, there's more because Bocuse lives in an age of high-speed trains and airplanes that have catapulted him into realms far beyond his own little world. He still advocates seasonal cuisine based on fresh market produce (he hates to see strawberries in winter and chestnuts in spring), but he serves nems without a qualm. In Florida, he invented the hamburger with foie gras and truffles. He travels everywhere, takes in everything around him. At L'Est, no one is surprised to see ham from Serrano served with foie gras from the Gers, or guacamole accompanying Cantonese rice and prawns. Bocuse's horizons have expanded, but he still views them from his home in Collonges.

THE STYLE

"Monsieur Paul, who does the cooking when you're not there? And you're not there a lot—yesterday you were in Sweden, tomorrow you'll be in Tokyo." The master snaps back, "The same people who do the cooking when I am there." In this case, Christian Bouvarel, who's been with Bocuse for thirty years and recently replaced Roger Jaloux, who held the position for thirty-eight years. Alfred, the maître d'hôtel, has manned his post for forty-five years. The people who work for Bocuse generally stay a long time.

Bocuse didn't place his kitchen team behind a big glass window in the Collonges restaurant merely for decorative purposes. He did it to underscore his belief that teamwork is more important than the inspiration of a single creative genius. He points out that Enzo Ferrari's cars are the finest in the world, despite the fact that Ferrari doesn't screw on every bolt with his own hands. Bocuse is an artist all right, but in the Renaissance sense of a man directing a studio of assistants. When Bocuse does put in an appearance—which happens more than people think—he eats with his guests. "If architects lived in the houses they design, they might design them better," he observes.

Bocuse's cuisine reflects an overall philosophy rather than a specific performance. Although he's one of the last remaining chefs to serve the classics—sole au beurre blanc, mussel soup, shoulder of veal stuffed with truffles and foie gras, this doesn't stop him from offering house specialties such as "chicken in mourning". The thing that pleases him most is simplicity. "There's only one rule: never put on a culinary show for its own sake. Our goal is to create a convivial atmosphere." A goal that has been amply achieved. Guests in the dining room include international gourmets, soccer players, visitors from Japan, people splurging on one great meal, businessmen, politicians. The disparate crowd often forges friendships over a cup of coffee after dessert; this is not the least of the many pleasures enjoyed by guests at Bocuse's table.

Facing page:
*L'Est, the brasserie housed in
the old Brotteaux railroad station.*

Above, top to bottom:
*Mint tea at Le Sud.
Frogs'-Legs Tempura at L'Ouest.
The Collonges' dishwashing staff.*

SERVES 4
- 1¼ lb raw red tuna
- 1 teaspoon wasabi paste (available from Asian groceries)
- ½ cup fish sauce
- ¾ cup olive oil & 4 tablespoons for the salad
- Juice of 2 limes
- 1 tablespoon soy sauce
- 1 teaspoon grilled sesame seeds
- ½ bunch coriander, chopped
- 10 oz rocket leaves (arugula)
- Juice of 1 lemon
- Ginger root in vinegar (available in Asian groceries)
- Salt, pepper

PREPARATION TIME
25 minutes

Raw Tuna Sashimi

SERVED AT *L'OUEST*, RECIPE BY FRÉDÉRIC BERTHOD FOR PAUL BOCUSE

In a bowl, beat together the wasabi, nuoc man, and olive oil. Add the lime juice and soy sauce. Season to taste and set aside.

Cut the tuna into thin slices about 1/5-inch (½ cm) thick. Pour some of the sauce onto four plates, top with slices of raw tuna, and finish with the remaining sauce. Sprinkle with the grilled sesame seeds and chopped coriander.

Garnish with rocket leaves that have been washed and seasoned with a dash of olive oil and lemon juice.

Serve chilled with ginger root in vinegar.

SERVES 4
- 16 frogs' legs
- 12 oz rocket leaves (arugula)
- 4 tablespoons olive oil
- Juice of 1 lemon
- Salt, pepper
- Oil for deep-fat fryer

For the tempura batter
- ¾ cup flour
- ¾ cup corn starch
- 1 teaspoon baking powder
- 1½ cups ice water
- ½ tablespoon peanut oil
- Pinch of red pepper
- Salt, pepper

PREPARATION TIME
35 minutes

COOKING TIME
10 minutes

Frogs'-Legs Tempura

SERVED AT *L'OUEST*, RECIPE BY FRÉDÉRIC BERTHOD FOR PAUL BOCUSE

Preheat oven to 400°F (200°C).

Beat all the tempura batter ingredients together in a bowl.

Cut the frogs' legs in two.

Ten minutes before serving, heat the oil in the deep-fat fryer to 325°F (160°C). Dip the frogs' legs in the batter and drop them into the hot oil four at a time. Cook for 8 minutes, stirring gently with a slotted spoon. Drain on absorbent paper and keep warm in the oven.

When all the frogs' legs are cooked, serve hot accompanied by a rocket salad seasoned with olive oil and lemon juice.

SERVES 4
• 16 raw prawns
• 8 sheets ready-to-bake
  phyllo dough
• 2 large carrots
• 5 oz celery root
• 5 oz fennel
• 3 oz black mushrooms
• 16 leaves fresh mint
• Salt, pepper
• Oil for deep-fat fryer

For the marinade
• ½ cup peanut oil
• 1 teaspoon curry paste
• 2 sprigs fresh coriander,
  chopped
• 1 clove garlic, chopped
• Salt, pepper

For the sauce
• 5 lumps sugar
• 10 tablespoons water
• ⅔ cup fish sauce
• 1 clove garlic, chopped
• 1 pinch red pepper flakes
• 1 carrot
• Salt, pepper

PREPARATION TIME
• 1 night in advance
• 45 minutes

COOKING TIME
10 minutes

The unique atmosphere of Le Sud.

Prawn Nems

SERVED AT *L'OUEST*, RECIPE BY FRÉDÉRIC BERTHOD FOR PAUL BOCUSE

• *The night before*: Combine all the ingredients for the marinade. Add the shelled prawns, cover with plastic film, and marinate overnight in the refrigerator.

• *Preparing the sauce*: Place the sugar and water in a pot. Boil over high heat until the mixture is lightly caramelized, remove from heat and add the fish sauce. Stir. Add the garlic, red pepper flakes, and carrot (pared and cut into julienne strips). Season to taste, stir, and chill.

Wash and pare the carrots and celery root, wash the fennel. Cut the vegetables into julienne strips. Finely chop the black mushrooms, add to the other vegetables.

Cut the sheets of phyllo dough in half. Place a mound of the vegetable mixture on each half-sheet of dough. Top with a rinsed mint leaf and 1 prawn. Roll into small cylinders and fold the ends over, completely enclosing the filling.

Heat the oil in the deep-fat fryer to 325°F (160°C). Drop the nems into the oil four-by-four. Cook until done, stirring occasionally with a slotted spoon. Drain on absorbent paper, and season to taste.

Glaze with the caramel sauce and serve hot.

SERVES 4
- 8 red mullet fillets weighing about 8 oz each
- ½ cup olive oil
- 1 lb potatoes
- 4 tablespoons butter
- 1 egg yolk
- 4 carrots
- 4 zucchini
- 1 cup white wine
- 1 cup Noilly Prat Vermouth
- 3 oz shallots
- 4 cups fish stock
- 2 cups crème fraîche
- 1 sprig fresh basil
- Salt, pepper

PREPARATION TIME
1 hour

COOKING TIME
20 minutes

Paul Bocuse is a staunch advocate of the chef's hat.

Fillets of Red Mullet with Potato Scales

SERVED AT *L'AUBERGE DE COLLONGES*

• *Preparing the sauce*: Peel the carrots and zucchini, and cut into small even cubes. Cook the vegetables in boiling salted water, refresh, drain, and dry in a clean cloth.

Place the white wine and Vermouth in a large pot. Pare and chop the shallot, add to the wine and reduce by one-half. Add the fish stock, whip with a wire whisk for 1 minute and simmer the sauce until reduced again, this time by one-third.

Add the crème fraîche and simmer until the sauce coats the back of a spoon. Season to taste, add the basil leaves, cover the pot with plastic film, and steep for 10 minutes at room temperature. Mix the sauce in the blender and strain into a clean pot. Add the cooked vegetables and keep hot in a pan of warm water.

Using tweezers, gently remove the bones from the fish fillets.

Pare the potatoes and cut into thin slices about 1/5-inch (½cm) thick. With a round cookie cutter, cut even disks out of each slice. Parboil the potato disks for 1 minute in boiling salted water. Drain and allow to cool at room temperature. When these potato "scales" are cool, mix with 1 tablespoon butter melted for 1 minute in the microwave.

In a bowl, beat the egg yolk with 1 teaspoon cold water. Using a pastry brush, smooth the egg-yolk coating over both sides of the fish fillets. Next, carefully cover the fillets with overlapping potato disks, working from the tail toward the head to produce a fish-scale effect. Place the fillets on a baking sheet and allow to rest for 30 minutes in the refrigerator.

Heat the olive oil in a large, nonstick frying pan. Place the fish fillets in the pan, potato side down, and brown gently in the oil for 6 to 8 minutes. Season the upper side of the fillets with salt and pepper, then carefully turn them over and brown for 5 minutes longer.

Serve 2 fillets per person on a base of warm sauce.

Il faut surprendre leurs rires... croire que les fumets et la mélodie du beurre blond entretiennent l'amour du beau. Qui a dit que Paul Bocuse a 75 ans ? Je ne le crois pas et je sais que le petit prince en le dessinant l'imaginait copain de classe.

... no stars, no ...
BOCUSE and no ...
comrades, copains, TROISG...
pranks straight out of kine...
fumets and beurre blond a...
Did someone say Paul Bo...
prince, le petit prince, wa...

Bresse "Chicken in Mourning" with Sauce Suprême

SERVED AT *L'AUBERGE DE COLLONGES*

• *Preparing the veal stuffing*: Place the veal in a food processor, season with salt and pepper, grind. Transfer the ground veal to a chilled bowl and blend with 5 tablespoons crème fraîche. Wash and peel the carrot, the turnip, and the celery root. Cut into cubes, cook in boiling salted water, refresh, and drain. In a separate pot of boiling salted water, cook the leek (white portion only) and the string beans. Cut the string beans into even pieces. Cut the foie gras and 2 of the truffle slices into small cubes. Blend all of the above ingredients, except for the leek, with the ground veal. Season to taste and set aside in the refrigerator.

• *Preparing the sauce suprême*: Melt the butter in a pot and blend with the flour. Allow to cool in the pot. Pour 1 quart boiling chicken stock into the pot, whipping constantly. Bring the sauce to the boil, continuing to whip. Add 5 tablespoons of crème fraîche. Season to taste and set aside.

Insert the remaining truffle slices under the skin of the chicken, on the breasts and thighs.

Fill the interior of the chicken with the veal-and-vegetable stuffing, placing the white portion of the leek in the center. Sew up the openings in the chicken. Place the chicken inside the pork bladder, add a pinch of salt and pepper and the Madeira. Close the bladder tightly and tie securely with string. Bring 5 quarts of chicken stock to the boil and place the chicken in it. Add water, if necessary, so the chicken is completely covered. Reduce the heat and simmer for 1 hour 30 minutes. When the chicken is cooked, drain it on a serving dish. Garnish with mounds of stuffing and serve with the reheated sauce suprême and rice. Carve the chicken, still in the pork bladder, at the table.

SERVES 4
• 1 Bresse chicken weighing about 4 lb (ask your butcher to clean and bone it through the back, leaving the wing and thigh bones attached)
• 4 quarts water
• 1 pork bladder (available from your pork butcher) soaked in salted water with vinegar

For the sauce suprême
• 2 tablespoons Madeira
• 5 tablespoons butter
• 5 tablespoons flour
• 5 tablespoons crème fraîche
• 6 quarts chicken stock
• Salt, pepper

For the veal stuffing
• 4 oz fillet of veal
• 5 tablespoons crème fraîche
• 1 carrot
• 2 oz turnips
• 2 oz celery root
• 1 leek (white portion only)
• 2 oz string beans
• 2 oz foie gras
• 8 slices fresh truffle

PREPARATION TIME
1 hour

COOKING TIME
1 hour 30 minutes

The frescoes at Collonges illustrate the history of cuisine in general, and Paul Bocuse in particular.

SERVES 4
• 1 Victoria pineapple
• 2 limes
• 2 cups sugar
• 2 cups water
• ½ cup Malibu (coconut liqueur)
• 1 tablespoon red berries
• 4 scoops lemon or pineapple sorbet

PREPARATION TIME
• 1 night in advance
• 35 minutes

COOKING TIME
30 minutes

Elegance in a contemporary mode.

Pineapple Carpaccio with Candied Lime Peel

SERVED AT *L'OUEST*, RECIPE BY FRÉDÉRIC BERTHOD FOR PAUL BOCUSE

• *The night before*: Peel the pineapple and carefully remove all the hard knots. Using a large sharp knife, cut the pineapple into very thin slices. Set aside in the refrigerator.

Peel the limes, and remove all white membrane from the peel. Cut the peel into julienne strips. Squeeze the juice into a medium-sized pot.

In another pot, boil the peel in water for 30 seconds. Change the water and boil again for another 30 seconds. Repeat, boiling 3 times in all.

Use 1/3 cup sugar and 1/4 cup water to make a syrup. Add the lemon rind and simmer gently until the rind is candied.

In a separate pot, blend 2 cups water with 2 cups sugar and bring to a boil. Remove from heat and add the Malibu (coconut liqueur), candied lemon rind, red berries, and lemon juice. Cool.

Add the pineapple slices to the syrup and allow to marinate for at least 12 hours.

The next day, place the pineapple slices on large plates. Cover with the syrup, garnish with the candied peel and place a scoop of sorbet in the center. Serve.

GÉRARD BOYER

THE MAN

Elegant and understated, the man resembles his domain. Gérard Boyer doesn't make a fuss when he welcomes you to Les Crayères. In good weather he'll seat you on the terrace overlooking an English-style park, with Reims Cathedral shimmering in the distance. His only comment? "This is a nice spot." In bad weather, guests wait in the armchairs dotted about a spacious solarium facing the forest, or under the brocade draperies of a bar that's full of light even on misty days. Boyer knows every detail of this décor by heart. "The house you see today has been completely transformed. My wife and I supervised the decoration ourselves, room by room."

Outdoors, servers glide with effortless grace over immaculately manicured lawns and gravel paths. Nestled in the gentle rolling countryside, the estate stands on a chalk knoll, or crayère, from which its name is derived. This chalky local soil is responsible for the fame of the region's foremost Champagne makers.

The location of Les Crayères—midway between town and country—is an aristocratic luxury. Indeed, the setting was chosen by aristocrats, but in fact not very long ago. Despite its eighteenth-century style, the château was actually built early in the twentieth century. To understand its history, visitors should cross the road and study the turrets, belfries, and battlements of the Pommery estate opposite. The Château des Crayères shares the same origin, since it was built by the Comtesse de Pommery and subsequently occupied by the Polignac family. Gérard Boyer converted it into a hotel-restaurant in 1983.

The château's new owner never ceases to be amazed by the many journeys that have brought him here. First, that of his grandfather, who left his native Auvergne and—faithful to tradition—opened a brasserie in Vincennes. Next, that of his father, who ran the family business before moving to Reims. "It was pure chance. He wanted to settle a hundred or so kilometers from Paris." This heralded the beginning of another

adventure, the inauguration of "La Chaumière," which propelled Boyer and his father into the upper echelon of great French chefs. "This craft is one of the last in which an indifferent schoolboy can attain the heights of achievement. The kitchen really is a ladder to social status."

From his Auvergnat roots and summers at his grandparents' farm, Boyer still remembers the smells of warm milk, damp earth, and freshly mown hay. This accounts for the natural ease he feels as master of the château.

Boyer's father recognized his son's vocation but, before allowing him to apprentice at some of France's best restaurants, including Lasserre, he put it to the test. Only someone with a genuine passion for the craft should ever dream of becoming a chef. The son passed with flying colors. "For me, the crucial revelation came when Paul Bocuse won his third Michelin star in 1965. I was leafing through the current issue of *Paris Match*, and came across an article featuring a man in a chef's hat and white coat. Suddenly, we all gained new status—and set ourselves new goals."

When the son returned to the family fold, his father wisely stepped aside. "There was never any conflict between us. He knew that sons inevitably replace their fathers in due course." And today, the master of Les Crayères gives full credit to his own chef. Thierry Voisin has followed in Boyer's footsteps for almost twenty years and is now his spiritual heir. A man entrusted with a precious legacy has an obligation to pass it on; to encourage the development of a new generation's avant-garde.

THE REGION

"We're right in the middle of the great invasion routes. This makes you want to pack your bags instead of getting out your pots and pans." Gérard Boyer sets the culinary tone himself. There are no forced allusions to the region on his menu. What would be the point? Until agriculture was revolutionized by the use of fertilizer, this region was so impoverished it was referred to as "wretched Champagne." In those days, its

Page 46:
The Chavot church rises from a vineyard in Champagne.

Page 47:
At Les Crayères, a temple dedicated to Champagne, glasses are etched with the initials of the estate's owner.

Left to right:
Sliced tomatoes in the sauté pan.
Brie with truffles, a house specialty.
An opportunity to rediscover the small suppliers of the Champagne region.

Facing page:
Rear view of the Pommery château, renamed Les Crayères by Gérard Boyer.

only treasure was a product easy to grow in poor soil: the lentil. Gérard Boyer does pay grudging homage to the tiny local red lentils, occasionally serving them puréed with squab. He gets sheep's-milk yogurt and strawberries from neighboring suppliers. Otherwise, he prefers working with France's more prestigious products, such as Challans duck and Bresse poultry. They may not be local, but their quality is superb. A dish such as Hare à la Royale is not associated with any particular region, but great cities enjoy the privilege of presenting the best France has to offer, and Reims is no exception. "This region has its own magic. It can't have been mere chance that led the Frankish king, Clovis, who was Belgian, to be baptized in Reims. And think of all the other sovereigns who chose Reims for their coronations. I do draw inspiration from the region. Not by scouring the countryside for local products and recipes; I am more like a painter working with the locale's distinctive light." In this he resembles all the artists from afar who have flocked to Champagne since the Middle Ages: ever since the court of the Pays d'Oc was overthrown by Thibaud and his followers.

The sky-lit bar installed by the Boyers.

Gérard Boyer may not emphasize the Champagne region in his cuisine, but Champagne wine is a different matter altogether. After sipping a preliminary glass of Champagne at aperitif time in the orangery, almost half of his guests order more Champagne with their dinner. They have 270 varieties to choose from, in addition to a selection of vintages including Bouzy, Ambonnay, and the other locally produced still red wines.

Champagne sparkles in the glass and also adds a special touch to sauces such as the one spooned over fillets of Saint Pierre (dory), generously accompanied with a leek-and-caviar torte. Champagne also determines the composition of the menu. "The decision to feature fish at my restaurant was a conscious one, since fish affords an opportunity to use Champagne in a host of interesting ways." Although indirect and subtle, this is a clear tribute to the spirit of the region.

THE STYLE

The château's décor calls for high style, and high style is the keynote. Dishes under silver covers are brought to the table by a corps of attentive servers executing an intricate minuet beneath the court portraits hanging on the walls above them. There's something Mozartian about the proceedings—brilliant and beguiling variations rung on familiar themes. Lightly smoked salmon, baked jacket potatoes with caviar cream, lobster cannelloni, two eggs scrambled with Iranian caviar: here is a world of luxury, stamped with Boyer's hallmark; stylish, but never intimidating.

Perfectly sautéed lamb chops are served with a simple garlic flan and eggplant caviar. The meal concludes with a pine-nut sand tart, but its essence is to be found elsewhere: in the skilled preparation of the lamb chops, in a host of tiny variations, in total mastery of the culinary craft. "Simplicity reflects a lifetime of experience. When an admiring young woman asked Picasso how long it took him to produce a painting, he replied, 'Forty years, madam.' I've spent all that time eliminating, condensing, cutting down. When you start out, you want to do well. You add things; you do too much. It's the sin of youth. With age, I've learned to do without the superfluous." Gérard Boyer knows, of course, that not all of his contemporaries follow the same principle, and that he, through this economy of means, belongs to a tradition of updated French classicism. He's proud of it. "People complain that globalization has brought conformity. Except in cuisine, where fusion has become a cliché."

Top to bottom:
François Laluc, a local producer, delivering sheep's-milk cheese.
Preparing for a feast.
Thierry Voisin (right), deep in conversation.

SERVES 4
- 20 large prawns, trimmed and shelled
- 2 hearts of lettuce
- 4 sprigs rosemary
- Oil for frying fritters

For the turmeric batter
- 3 tablespoons flour
- 1 teaspoon baking powder
- 3 tablespoons potato flour
- 1 egg
- ½ cup milk
- 1 teaspoon turmeric
- 1 tablespoon fleur de sel

For the "tacos"
- 6 sheets ravioli (or lasagna) dough
- ½ lb fresh goat's cheese
- 2 tablespoons shelled prawn meat chopped in a food processor
- ½ cup olive oil
- A few cumin seeds
- ½ bunch chives, chopped
- Salt, pepper

For the rosemary mixture
- 2 oz phyllo dough with 2 sprigs chopped rosemary

For the cardamom mixture
- 3 tablespoons breadcrumbs mixed with a pinch of chopped cardamom
- Salt, pepper

PREPARATION TIME
1 hour

COOKING TIME
15 minutes

Trio of Spiced Prawns with Goat's-Cheese Tacos

- *Preparing the "tacos"*: Using a pair of scissors, carefully cut the ravioli dough into 16 identical pieces. Spread the squares of ravioli dough on a baking sheet, dry out for 4 minutes in the oven, cool. Whip the goat's cheese with the prawn meat, season to taste, add the olive oil, cumin, and chives. Blend well, correct seasoning.

Make 4 "tacos" by spreading the fresh goat's cheese mixture between layers of the dried ravioli dough. Place on serving plates with a few lettuce leaves.

Preheat oven to 400°F (200°C).

Place all the ingredients for the turmeric batter in a bowl, whisk until smooth.

Dredge 12 prawns in the rosemary mixture and deep-fry for 5 minutes, stirring constantly. Thread onto sprigs of rosemary.

Dredge 4 prawns in the cardamom mixture, deep-fry for 5 minutes, and arrange on plates. Lastly, dip the 4 remaining prawns in the turmeric batter, deep-fry, then drain on absorbent paper and serve hot.

Kitchen strainer.

Mousseline of Red Peppers, Puréed Herbs, and Deep-Fried Prawns in an Orange-Flavored Crust

Preheat oven to 350°F (180°C).

Peel the orange using a carrot scraper, and cut into julienne strips. Squeeze the juice of the orange into a bowl and set aside for use in the herb oil. Simmer the orange peel in 4 changes of water and mix with the sesame seeds. Add the mixture to the breadcrumbs and set aside.

• *Preparing the pepper purée*: Rub the peppers with olive oil and roast for 30 minutes. Remove from oven and peel. Remove the seeds and membrane from the peppers and chop. Sauté the chopped peppers with the peeled and chopped onion in ½ cup hot olive oil. Add the chopped clove of garlic and simmer for 10 minutes, stirring constantly. Season to taste, add the cream, bring to the boil, and mix in blender.

• *Preparing the herb oil*: Wash the fresh herbs and remove the leaves. Mix the leaves in a food processor with the lime juice, orange juice, and ½ cup olive oil.

Peel the prawns and dip in milk, then in the beaten egg, and lastly in the breadcrumb, sesame seed, and orange peel mixture. Deep-fry the prawns two-by-two, stirring constantly. Drain on a clean towel.

Fill small individual parfait glasses, starting with the herb oil, then the pepper purée, and ending with a lukewarm prawn. This dish may be accompanied with toast or small puff pastries.

SERVES 4
- 4 medium prawns
- ⅓ cup milk
- 1 egg, beaten
- Salt, pepper
- Oil for deep-fat frying
- 1 orange
- 1 teaspoon grilled sesame seeds
- ½ cup breadcrumbs

For the pepper purée
- 2 red peppers
- 1 onion
- ½ cup olive oil
- 1 clove garlic
- ½ cup heavy cream

For the herb oil
- 1 bunch basil
- ½ bunch tarragon
- ½ bunch chervil
- Juice of 1 lime
- ½ cup olive oil

PREPARATION TIME
25 minutes

COOKING TIME
10 minutes

Zucchini Fritters

Place all the ingredients for the fritter batter in a bowl. Beat until smooth.

Cut the zucchini into even slices about 1/5 inch (½ cm) thick. Dip the slices in the fritter batter and fry four-by-four in fairly hot oil. Drain on absorbent paper.

Season the fritters with fleur de sel and serve at aperitif time or as a garnish for fish or grilled meat.

SERVES 4
- 4 tender young zucchini
- Oil for deep-fat frying

For the fritter batter
- 3 tablespoons flour
- 1 teaspoon baking powder
- 3 tablespoons potato flour
- 1 egg
- ½ cup milk
- 1 tablespoon fleur de sel

PREPARATION TIME
35 minutes

COOKING TIME
15 minutes

Page 56:
Zucchini fritters.

Page 57:
It will soon be harvest-time in the region between Brie and Champagne.

SERVES 4
For the pigs' feet
- 5 oz carrots
- 1 rib celery
- 1 onion
- ½ leek
- 5 tablespoons goose grease & 3 tablespoons for cooking the pigs' feet
- 1 lb red Champagne lentils (or Puy lentils)
- 1 cup chicken stock
- Salt, pepper
- 4 pigs' feet simmered in stock for 2 hours, boned
- 5 oz foie gras
- 1 lb thin sheets pork fat from the stomach lining
- 1 cup red wine
- ½ cup Madeira
- 2 cups cooking liquid from the pigs' feet

For the vinaigrette
- 2 tablespoons sherry vinegar
- 3 tablespoons walnut oil
- 6 tablespoons truffle oil
- 1 oz chopped truffles
- Salt, pepper

PREPARATION TIME
2 hours

COOKING TIME
3 hours

Truffle slicer.

Braised Pigs' Feet Stuffed with Foie Gras on a Bed of Red Champagne Lentils and Truffle Vinaigrette

Peel, wash, and coarsely chop the carrots, celery, and onion. Wash and coarsely slice the leek. Melt 5 tablespoons goose grease in a large pot, add the vegetables and allow to wilt for 5 minutes. Add the lentils and the stock. Simmer for about 45 minutes, stirring occasionally. Drain off any remaining liquid and keep warm.

Bone the pigs' feet. On a flat surface, spread out 4 large sheets of pork caul. Place one pigs' foot in the center of each sheet, top with an oblong of foie gras arranged lengthwise. Roll tightly and fold the ends under, forming small airtight cylinders.

Melt the remaining goose grease in a flameproof casserole. Brown the cylinders evenly on all sides in the hot grease.

Add the red wine, reduce by one-half. Add the Madeira and cooking liquid from the pigs' feet.

Simmer for 1 hour, basting occasionally.

Add the lentils to the casserole and cook for 30 minutes more, making sure the lentils do not stick to the bottom of the casserole.

Stir the vinaigrette ingredients together in a bowl.

Pour the vinaigrette over the pigs' feet and serve directly from the casserole.

Sautéed Sliced Veal Kidneys, Quick-Cooked Spinach, Foie-Gras Flan, and Pan Gravy with Sherry

• *Preparing the foie-gras flan*: Grease small molds (demi-tasse cups or small aluminum molds) with the butter, going over them twice. Chill in refrigerator. In a bowl, whip together the foie-gras purée, crème fraîche, heavy cream, and egg. Pour this mixture into the chilled molds, and place the molds in a pan of hot water. Bake for 30 minutes at 300°F (150°C).

• *Preparing the sherry sauce*: Sweat the mushrooms in the butter. Add the sherry. Simmer reducing the sherry by one-half. Add the veal stock and continue to simmer, this time reducing the liquid by three-quarters. Correct the seasoning and set aside in a pan of warm water.

• *Preparing the roasted shallots*: Wash the gray shallots, wrap in aluminum foil with a little butter, and bake for 40 minutes.

• *Preparing the wine butter*: Peel and chop the gray shallot. Melt the butter in a saucepan, add the shallot and wilt for 5 minutes without coloring. Add the red wine and reduce until there is almost nothing left. Remove from heat, cool, add the 10 tablespoons butter and whip. Set this wine butter aside at room temperature.

• *Preparing the kidneys*: Cut the kidneys into slices about ⅓-inch (1 cm) thick. Sear the kidneys in 5 tablespoons butter, drain, and place in a large earthenware baking dish. Cover each slice with wine butter and finish cooking in the oven to the degree of doneness you prefer. Just before serving, quick-cook the spinach in 4 tablespoons butter. Season to taste.

Arrange slices of kidney on large plates, garnish with a roasted shallot split in two and a small mound of spinach. Place an unmolded foie-gras flan on top of each mound of spinach. Heat the sherry sauce and whip in 5 tablespoons butter cut into small pieces. Pour a little sauce around each plate and serve.

SERVES 4
• 2 trimmed veal kidneys
• 5–6 oz fresh spinach
• 4 large gray shallots
• 5 tablespoons butter for cooking the kidneys & 4 tablespoons for cooking the spinach

For the sherry sauce
• 1 cup sherry
• 1 cup veal stock
• 5 tablespoons butter
• 2 oz mushrooms

For the foie-gras flan
• 4½ oz raw foie gras puréed in a food processor and put through a strainer
• 1 tablespoon crème fraîche
• ⅓ cup heavy cream
• 1 egg
• 1 teaspoon cognac
• 3 tablespoons softened butter for greasing the molds
• Salt, pepper

For the wine butter
• 1 gray shallot
• ⅓ cup red wine
• 10 tablespoons butter

PREPARATION TIME
1 hour 30 minutes

COOKING TIME
1 hour 30 minutes

A street in Reims named after Gérard's father.

SERVES 4
For the crème brûlée
- 5 egg yolks
- 4 tablespoons sugar
- 2 cups heavy cream
- 3 tablespoons fresh truffles, chopped
- 4 tablespoons brown sugar for the crust

For the chocolate cake
- 4 tablespoons cooking chocolate (70 percent cocoa content)
- 2 eggs & 1 yolk
- 3 tablespoons sugar
- ½ teaspoon baking powder
- 3 tablespoons flour
- 1 tablespoon cocoa
- 5 tablespoons softened butter & 3 tablespoons for the molds
- 4 cups port wine simmered until reduced by one-half

PREPARATION TIME
1 hour

COOKING TIME
10 minutes

In the kitchen.

Crème Brûlée with Black Truffles and Warm, Tender Chocolate Cake served with Port-Wine sauce and Chocolate Sorbet

• *Preparing the crème brûlée*: Preheat oven to 160°F(70°C). In a large bowl, beat the egg yolks with the sugar until smooth. Add the heavy cream and the truffles. Mold the cream in the hollows of 4 soup plates. Cut a small circle in the center of each molded cream and sprinkle with the brown sugar. Bake for 1 hour. Cool, cover with plastic film, and allow to rest.

• *Preparing the chocolate cake*: Preheat oven to 300°F (200°C). Melt the chocolate. In a large bowl, mix the 2 eggs and 1 yolk with the sugar. When the batter is smooth, add the baking powder, flour, cocoa, melted chocolate, and softened butter. Grease 4 small ramekins with the remaining butter. Fill the molds up to halfway with the batter and bake for 4 minutes.

Caramelize the custard in the bowls with a salamander or under a very hot broiler.

Gently remove the chocolate cakes from the ramekins while still warm. Place them in the center of the caramelized custards and pour the port-wine reduction around them. Serve immediately to underscore the contrast between the warm cake and the cool custard. This dessert may be accompanied with chocolate sorbet or ice cream.

ARNAUD DAGUIN

LES PLATANES

BIARRITZ

THE MAN

He learned all he needed to know about winning stars and managing a business, about
dealing with food critics ready to pounce on the smallest error, and about handling
employees who have to be kept on their toes, pushed around, dispensed with. Then
he packed up and left. He didn't go far. He stayed in his native region, the southwest
of France, but now he's at peace, no longer haunted by family memories, at ease beneath
the plane trees of Biarritz. Standing contentedly in the doorway of his restaurant, he
doesn't even yearn for the beach or the glamor of the Casino and the Grand Hôtel. All
he wants is this tranquil neighborhood where people come for him, and him alone.

His family lives on the upper floor. His wife Véronique manages the dining room.
He works behind the scenes, with just one assistant and someone to clean up. He
claims his cuisine wouldn't be the same if he'd never met Véronique. She sets the tone
in his world. Thus, with each new day, Arnaud Daguin can revel in the luxury of
inventing and improvising, of deciding on his menu only after he's returned from market, of building it around the products he found there and around his own mood.

He describes himself as the survivor of a hard-fought battle for freedom. It was
hard to erase the image of his father, André Daguin, a chef famed throughout the
Southwest. André was a man whose own father ran a restaurant, a man trained in the
old school, a man who worked as a chef on the Compagnie des Wagons Lits dining
cars at a time when they were traveling embassies for French cuisine. He was an inventive man, nonetheless. Lightly sautéed breast of duck served rare was his idea, and he
elevated a dish that was once only eaten preserved to the status of jewel in the crown
of musketeer-country gastronomy. André Daguin also stood out as a recognized master of foie gras and wood pigeon at Auch's Hôtel de France, a temple of gastronomy
in its time. Today Arnaud's voluble father has shifted gears and now serves as
spokesman for the French restaurant trade.

As a member of this talented and demanding family, Arnaud had to fight to make himself heard. He recalls being pushed into the kitchen on Wednesday afternoons, when there is no school in France, and forced to assist the family restaurant's aging chef. "He scared me to death, he yelled, he threw pots. But I learned all the basics from him without setting foot in cookery school." Arnaud went to college in Paris and then completed a training program in Washington, D.C. He spent a long time considering his options: dance, theater, just having a good time. Anything to stay out of the kitchen. "Everyone expected me to go back to cooking, and it's tough to have your whole life mapped out for you when you're only twenty years old." But back he went. He took over at his father's for a while, but the two men never saw eye-to-eye and tempers flared. Arnaud decided to strike out on his own. Differently. "I didn't want to head a huge staff any more. I was tired of worrying that if I turned my back for a moment, someone would stick a knife into it."

At Biarritz he can relax and take his time. With seating for just twenty, he doesn't have to work as if he were on an assembly line. And he also understands, at last, what the craft of fine cooking really amounts to. "It's not pure art. There are too many rules, too much repetition. Even if I change the menu every day, I still have to reproduce the same recipe fifteen, twenty times. And I'm dealing with perishable products. Once you take a scallop out of its shell, the countdown begins." Not pure art, perhaps. But great art just the same.

THE REGION

Daguin's corner of the French Southwest, the Gers, is earthy—corn-fed geese, hunters in the woods on Sunday. In the Basque country, he's had to give some thought to the sea and its bounty. Along with the foie gras he grew up with, his menu now features fresh seafood and prawns. The prawns come straight from an ocean-side hatchery, and he uses them to make a soup garnished with…prawns. Heads for the broth, tails added whole. Heads and tails—a gourmet winner.

Left to right:
Tomme, a famed
Basque specialty.
A flock of wild geese overhead
—a moment to treasure.
Chicken foie gras,
a house specialty.

Arnaud has very definite ideas about the products he uses. Ham? He likes thick slices cut from hams dried in the cellar of a peasant who lives in the nearby mountains. "Salting and aging the ham is a whole chapter of cuisine in itself." Chicken? Preferably nineteen weeks old, so it stays firm when cooked. "My local poultry-man was factory-farming his birds, but I encouraged him to try traditional methods. He doesn't regret the change. Now his poultry is plump and tender, the best in the region." Mushrooms? Only in season. Arnaud is no fan of cans and bottles. As for the famed peppers from Espelette, a village near the farmhouse he purchased recently, he uses them but doesn't make a fuss about it. "It's an excellent condiment, but if I couldn't get ahold of any, frankly my cuisine wouldn't suffer unduly."

Arnaud Daguin admires natural production methods. "The history of foie gras began when a hunter noticed that geese fatten themselves in autumn in order to survive the long migration ahead. Their livers become enlarged and more flavorful. Could this be done systematically, by farmers? In all seasons? The whole history of foie gras is summed up in these early experiments. I never tire of foie gras." He also never tires of chocolate, which has made his desserts famous. This is a tribute to local tradition, since chocolate—once exported from America to Bayonne—is intimately linked with the region's history. It's also a whole philosophy. "Chocolate is a miracle, just like foie gras. Nothing could be more unappetizing than a cacao pod. As long as the bean remained inside, as long as the bean wasn't fermented, roasted, and refined, as long as no one had the brilliant idea of making a paste with the butter extracted from it, it was worthless. It takes human genius to improve on nature."

The Biarritz shoreline.

Page 68:
Here, kids play pelota as naturally as they do soccer.

Page 69:
Pigeons: highly symbolic for Arnaud Daguin.

THE STYLE

Daguin's specialty is boned pigeon. "I must have boned 15,000 pigeons in my time. When I first started out, it took me fifteen minutes per bird. Today I can do the job in two-and-a-half minutes flat." This gives him precious extra minutes for thinking about the next step. The stuffing is made from squash, chestnuts, foie gras, or truffles. Boning a pigeon is just a technique anyone can learn. It's what comes afterward that matters, the thousands of things you can do once the bones are out. Daguin learned his boning technique in traditional kitchens, but what he does to the bird afterward is his own invention.

As a rule, Arnaud Daguin never follows a recipe. He works by instinct, on the inspiration of the moment, adding his personal touch without endless preliminaries: "Like a writer who gets it right the first time, and doesn't bother with rough drafts." Just the opposite of someone like Ferran-Adrian, the inspired Catalonian at El Bullit to whom Daguin refers frequently with respect. "His cuisine is conceptual. A succession of flavors and textures that's almost abstract. What I try to do is bring out the true essence of a product."

There's nothing new about this idea, as he admits. But it takes a little explaining: it doesn't mean the product should be left alone. "A plain grilled fish is totally uninteresting." The fish needs to be enhanced without masking its inherent nature. "Three flavors on the plate, no more. My approach to foie gras is to set off its basic flavor and texture by accompanying it with a vegetable for crisp contrast, and a condiment that brings out the flavor of both."

Facing page:
A family enterprise under
the plane trees.

Right:
A day off at the farm.

Far right:
Basque peppers—red or green,
sweet or hot.

Cream of Prawn Soup

SERVES 4
- 16 very fresh prawns
- 3 tablespoons fresh Tarbe beans
- ½ pound celery root
- 4 salsify roots
- Oil for deep-fat fryer
- 4 tablespoons olive oil & 2 tablespoons olive oil for cooking the prawns
- 1 shallot, peeled and chopped
- 1 clove garlic with skin, crushed
- 1 cup fish stock
- Salt, pepper

PREPARATION TIME
1 hour

COOKING TIME
30 minutes

Shell the beans and cook in boiling water. Drain. Season to taste, add a teaspoon of water, and blend in the food processor.

Trim the celery root and cut into pieces about 2 inches in diameter. Cook in boiling salted water, drain, and keep warm in a little fish stock.

Pare and cut the salsify roots into thin slices. Deep fry the slices for 3 minutes, stirring constantly. When the salsify slices are golden, drain on absorbent paper and keep warm.

Shell the prawns, reserving the shells and heads.

In a large pot, heat the olive oil to smoking point. Place the prawn shells and heads in the smoking oil, stirring constantly. Add the shallot and the crushed garlic.

Lower the heat and continue cooking for 2 minutes. Add the fish stock, season to taste, and simmer for 30 minutes.

To make the velouté, add the puréed beans to the broth, bring to a boil, stir with a wire whip, remove from heat, strain through a fine sieve, and keep warm.

Season the shelled prawns and sauté in olive oil for 1 minute on each side.

Arrange the sautéed prawns in large soup plates with the celery root. Cover with the boiling velouté. Garnish with the deep-fried salsify slices. Serve.

Creamed Watercress with Sea Scallops

SERVES 4
- 2 bunches watercress
- 3 tablespoons butter
- 1 cup heavy cream
- Salt, pepper
- 24 sea scallops
- ¼ cup olive oil

PREPARATION TIME
30 minutes

COOKING TIME
5 minutes

Wash and stem the watercress, chop the leaves coarsely. Melt the butter, add the watercress leaves and cook until wilted. Add the cream, boil for 2 minutes, season to taste and purée in a blender.

Heat the olive oil in a frying pan, sauté the sea scallops.

Reheat the creamed watercress, garnish with the sea scallops, and serve.

Page 74:
Checking the glasses.

Page 75:
Creamed watercress with sea scallops.

SERVES 4
- 4 pieces of raw duck foie gras (about 5 oz each)
- 4 large mushrooms
- 1 lb fresh spinach
- 4 tablespoons lightly salted butter
- 1 clove garlic with skin, crushed
- Salt, pepper
- 4 teaspoons sherry vinegar
- Coarse Guérande salt

PREPARATION TIME
35 minutes

COOKING TIME
20 minutes

Poached Duck Foie Gras with Tender Young Spinach

Wash and stem the mushrooms. Place in an ungreased frying pan over medium heat and sear for 5 minutes until brown, almost "burned." Keep warm on back of stove or in oven.

Trim the spinach and rinse in plenty of water. Wrap in a clean cloth to dry. Melt the butter in a large frying pan, add the garlic and spinach, and stir-fry for 2 minutes. Season to taste, drain, and keep warm.

Ten minutes before serving, scald the foie gras by dropping the pieces one-by-one into a pot of boiling salted water. Next, place in microwave oven (at 500 W) for 30 seconds.

To assemble: arrange the pieces of warm foie gras on plates, add the spinach and one chopped mushroom cap. Pour one tablespoon of sherry vinegar over each piece of foie gras, season with coarse salt.

Basque pasturelands.

SERVES 4
- 4 fillets of meagre (sea bass and tuna are also suitable for this recipe) weighing about 6 oz each
- 6 large Brittany artichokes
- Juice of 1 lemon
- 6 tablespoons olive oil & 4 tablespoons for cooking the fish
- Oil for deep-fat fryer
- Salt, pepper, fleur de sel

PREPARATION TIME
45 minutes

COOKING TIME
45 minutes

An artichoke brings the taste of Brittany to a cuisine based on southern flavors.

Sautéed Meagre Fillets with Artichokes in Olive Oil

Cut off the tips and stems of the artichokes. Using a sharp paring knife, work in a circular motion to cut the leaves away from the choke (hairy center) and bottom of each artichoke. Sprinkle the artichoke hearts with lemon juice to prevent discoloration. Place two raw artichoke hearts in a bowl of cold water with a dash of lemon juice. Drop the four others in boiling water with a little lemon juice. Cook until tender, checking after 20 minutes. When fully cooked, drain and rinse under cold water. Remove chokes.

Place the artichoke bottoms in a bowl and mash with a fork. Add the 6 tablespoons of olive oil, season to taste and mix into a coarse purée.

Heat the oil in the deep-fat fryer. Drain the two raw artichoke bottoms, remove the chokes, and wipe dry. Cut into very thin, even slices and fry for 5 minutes in the hot oil until golden. Drain on absorbent paper, season with fleur de sel, and keep warm.

Salt the fish fillets, heat the remaining olive oil in a non-stick frying pan, and sauté the fillets for 3 minutes on each side.

Reheat the artichoke purée for 3 minutes in the microwave. Scoop the purée onto the plates, top with the meagre fillets, and garnish with the fried artichoke slices.

SERVES 4
- 4 fairly firm white peaches
- 1 cup granulated sugar
- 1 cup water
- 3 vanilla pods
- 10 lumps sugar
- 4 tablespoons cold water
- 1 sheet ovenproof paper
- 1 teaspoon peanut oil
- 1 cup very fresh heavy cream
- 1 tablespoon confectioners' sugar

For the caramelized pastry
- 1 lb ready-to-bake puff pasty
- ½ cup confectioners' sugar

PREPARATION TIME
1 hour, beginning the night before serving

COOKING TIME
1 hour

The Biarritz beach as seen from the Grand Hôtel.

Peaches in Caramelized Pastry

• *Preparing the peaches (the night before)*: Stem the peaches and scald for 3 minutes in a large pot of boiling water. Drain, and refresh under a stream of cold water. Using the tip of a paring knife, carefully peel the peaches. Mix 1 cup granulated sugar with 1 cup water and 1 vanilla pod split in two. Cook for 10 minutes, or until the mixtures forms a syrup. Drop the peaches into the syrup and poach over a low heat until the peach flesh separates from the pit. When the peaches are cooked, tender but still slightly firm, remove from heat and allow to cool in the syrup.

• *Preparing the pastry*: Preheat oven to 350°. Roll the puff pastry out on a large cookie sheet, cover with a rack so that it will rise evenly, and bake for 20 minutes. Remove the cooked pastry from the oven, dredge with confectioners' sugar and return to oven for about 10 minutes, until crusty and golden. Allow the pastry to cool slightly and then use a large serrated knife to cut it into 8 identical sections.

Place the lumps of sugar in a small pot with the 4 tablespoons of water. Heat without stirring over medium heat until a light caramel is formed. Remove from heat and cool by placing the pot in a bowl of cold water. Stir the caramel occasionally with a fork. When the cooled caramel forms a thread on the fork, place it on a piece of oiled ovenproof paper and use the tines of the fork to pull it out into long threads of "angel hair."

Split the 2 remaining vanilla pods in two, scrape the seeds into the heavy cream, add the husks. Add a tablespoon of confectioners' sugar and whip until firm.

Arrange two peach halves on each of four puff-pastry rectangles. Spread with whipped cream and cover with the remaining four rectangles. Garnish with the angel hair and serve immediately.

MARC HAEBERLIN

L'AUBERGE DE L'ILL

ILLHAUSERN

THE MAN

When he was a boy, Marc Haeberlin built his playhouses out of crates he stole from his father. Wooden lobster crates made from forest oak, redolent with the scent of the sea. He also played on the terrace of his family's restaurant, blissfully unaware that princes and statesmen were dining just behind him. When he was older, he dreamt of being a farmer or gamekeeper so he could stay close to nature. He ended up putting nature on a dinner plate.

Did he really have a choice? The Haeberlins have always ended up in the kitchen. Marc's father Paul learned cooking from his father, who learned it from his father. Marc's uncle Jean-Pierre followed the same path. Although trained as an interior designer/architect, he spent his whole career in the restaurant. This joint endeavor, with the entire family living and working, until recently, under the same roof, spared neither young nor old. Marc himself has children and nephews who are already expressing an interest in the field. "My grandmother lived a short distance from the inn. When she felt her end was near, she called in the whole staff, not just the family. She thanked them all and then, ten minutes later, she died."

Haeberlin has a timeless quality: he is a man living in the continuum of succeeding generations, as fluid as the River Ill, which runs beneath his window. He apprenticed all over France with the best chefs of his time: Bocuse, Lasserre, Troisgros. "On my first night in Roanne, across from the railroad station, I kept staring at the Troisgros sign. I couldn't believe I was really there." But he subsequently returned to his point of departure, to the imposing house that will soon celebrate its 150th anniversary.

The house has actually had two lives. During its first life it was L'Arbre Vert, a generous riverbank table d'hôte where female cooks prepared game and eel stews. In good weather the tables were moved outdoors and set up under a stately weeping-willow tree: a tranquil village life at the foot of the wooden bridge. Then came the Second World War.

A bombing raid demolished everything—the bridge, the house, the old weeping willow. The family had to choose between leaving or rebuilding. Paul and Jean-Pierre decided to rebuild.

By a stroke of luck, they found an old half-timbered house with a steep pointed roof dating from 1578 that they could move onto their own land. They dug in their heels and determined to set their sights high. This marked the beginning of the house's second life, one that continues to this day. Uncle Jean-Pierre—impeccably turned out, the Order of Merit pinned to his lapel, his facial expression borrowed from the French actor Louis Jouvet—personally greets each guest on the threshold of the dining room. Paul, now over eighty years old, still wears his white chef's coat. His son has retained the stars he won. Everything is just the same, and yet everything is constantly changing through small successive adjustments, which is the way Marc likes to do it. "Demands aren't the same, tastes change. When we earned our third star, we were still serving melon with port and shrimp avocado…." The very status of the chef has been revolutionized. "When my father was awarded his third star, it didn't even rate a mention in the local newspaper. Today, reporters call me for interviews all the time."

Marc may be famous, but he's faithful to his roots. On Good Fridays he still serves fish stew, and after Sunday mass the villagers are welcome in his salon for an apéritif, a tradition dating from the days of L'Arbre Vert.

THE REGION

Marc's father served four terms as mayor of the village. Marc himself speaks Alsatian and pays ample tribute to the region in his books. Like all of his peers, he uses Périgord truffles and Brittany lobsters, but he's careful to give his menu a regional slant.

There's cabbage, for example: plump fresh heads of cabbage from the local vegetable man, sauerkraut from Krautergersheim ("Cabbagetown," in Alsatian). There's the carp, perch, pike, salmon, and eel that Adrien, one of the last professional fishermen in the area,

Left to right:
The chef's own sweet-brier jam is
available for sale at the hotel.
One of the hotel's windows.
The foie gras is served with a
spoon, as it used to be in Alsace.

Facing page:
A batch of pretzels.

still hauls into his boat from nets cast in the Rhine and its tributaries. There are pheasants and hares, which village friends hunt for him in season. Marc himself is a connoisseur of game: he learned how to hunt from his maternal grandfather, an expert. There are Alsatian wines too, of course: 150 of them on the wine list. Many more await discovery by Serge Dubs, one of the world's best wine stewards, who has been advising customers at the restaurant for twenty years. When Marc Haeberlin composes his menu, he draws inspiration from his native soil.

But there's no "local color" in his cuisine. It's more a matter of subtle allusion, nostalgic reminiscence. A bed of red cabbage—simple peasant fare—served with a delicately lacquered mallard duck. Or *knepfla*, the little dumplings that were once seen on every table, served with stewed dried fruit (the best kind, in winter) to accompany venison. Another local specialty is sliced gingerbread, drenched in citrus-fruit salad and topped with beer ice cream. Many dishes are slightly spicy. "Alsace was once on a major trade route. A land of markets and merchants, with a Jewish community that contributed a central-European note to local cooking." A region, like its cuisine, that is open to the world outside.

THE STYLE

Take foie gras, for example. An eminently local product, with all due respect to the musketeers of the Southwest. The drawings by the Alsatian illustrator Jean Jacques Waltz, known as Hansi, prove it: the courtyards of his farms are always full of geese. Marc serves foie gras rare, lukewarm, and perfectly tender. He accompanies it with navy beans, a salad of minced tripe, and a mousseline of truffles—a vegetable once fed to pigs. Cheap and hearty tripe, the rare and sophisticated truffle: a combination of opposites, from peasant to patrician fare. "I like to play in different keys. To combine a whole truffle with mashed potatoes, garnish a dish of sturgeon and sauerkraut with caviar butter." This annoys Marc's father, who considers his son's innovations a little outlandish,

Page 86:
One of the hotel's newly
decorated rooms.

Page 87:
A kitchen apprentice benefits
from learning on the job.

Left to right:
Gugelhopf dough rising.
A chef faithful to his post.
Peaches in syrup, the basis for a
classic invented by Paul's father
(recipe page 98).

but the elder Haeberlin doesn't hold it against the younger. His son has talent and the family knows it.

An array of fruit purées.

And respect for his father. His menu still lists the great dishes responsible for Paul's fame: Smoked Salmon Soufflé, Mousseline of Frogs' Legs, Hare à la Royale. Edouard Weber, former chef to the Romanovs in Saint Petersburg and mentor to the elder Haeberlin, still rates a mention. Marc's sole-and-lobster timbale is made according to the original recipe. All the classics are served unchanged, as a matter of fact. "I just reduced the quantities a little to adapt them to modern appetites." Otherwise, Marc composes his menus in his own way, which is creative but not revolutionary. "I hate it when someone puts a plate in front of me and says, 'Taste this, then I'll tell you what it is.' I want to recognize what I'm eating. Also, you can use traditional techniques and still impress people." A feat he achieves with each mouthful, through an accumulation of details, a lavish finesse.

SERVES 4
- ¾ lb boned, skinned fresh salmon
- ¾ lb smoked salmon
- 2 gray shallots, peeled and chopped
- 3 tablespoons wine vinegar
- 6 tablespoons olive oil
- Ground Espelette red pepper
- 4 eggs
- 2 tablespoons distilled vinegar
- 1 heart curly chicory lettuce
- 4 tablespoons smoked herring roe
- 4 tablespoons trout roe
- ⅔ cup crème fraîche
- Salt, pepper

For the pancakes
- ½ cup heavy cream
- 1 teaspoon salt
- 5 tablespoons flour
- 2 tablespoons water
- 2 tablespoons white wine
- 1 teaspoon kirsch

PREPARATION TIME
45 minutes

COOKING TIME
25 minutes

A trompe-l'œil crayfish under the window.

Poached Egg in Pancake Pockets on a Tartare of Marinated Fresh and Smoked Salmon with Herring Roe

• *Preparing the pancakes*: Proceed as for standard crêpe batter. Place the dry ingredients in a bowl. Add the liquid ingredients gradually, in order to avoid lumps, whipping with a wire whisk until blended. Cook the pancakes (one per serving) in a greased or oiled utensil designed for the purpose, or in a small non-stick frying pan. To prevent the pancakes from browning, use only a small amount of grease or oil. The pancakes should be thin and delicate. Set the cooked pancakes aside in a warm place and allow to dry slightly.

Shred the fresh and smoked salmon. Mix with the shallots, wine vinegar, and olive oil. Season to taste, add a pinch of ground Espelette red pepper.

Poach the eggs one-by-one in simmering water with the distilled vinegar. Drain on a cloth.

Place mounds of the salmon mixture on serving plates. Split the pancakes into two. Place one piece on the salmon, top with the poached egg, and finish with the second piece.

Garnish the edges of the plate with the lettuce and fish roe, decorate with a spoonful of whipped crème fraîche, and serve.

Paul Haeberlin's Mousseline of Frogs' Legs

• *Preparing the frogs' legs*: Melt 2 tablespoons butter in a frying pan, add 4 peeled chopped shallots and cook over low heat until wilted. Add half of the frogs' legs, cover with the Riesling, season to taste, and simmer for 10 minutes. Remove the frogs' legs from the pan and drain. Strain the pan juices and reduce by one-half over low heat.

• *Preparing the frogs'-leg mousse*: Bone the remainder of the frogs' legs. Chop the meat, add the flaked pike and mix in blender. Add the egg whites and continue mixing while gradually adding an equal amount of crème fraîche. Season to taste. When the mousse is smooth and thoroughly blended, remove and transfer to a terrine.

• *Preparing the spinach*: Stem and rinse the spinach, cook for 5 minutes in a pot of boiling salted water. Drain in a colander and press to squeeze out the moisture. Melt 3 tablespoons butter in a frying pan, crush the garlic and add. When the butter begins to foam, add the spinach, season to taste and heat for 5 minutes, stirring constantly.

• *Preparing the tomato purée*: Trim the tomatoes and immerse for 1 minute in boiling salted water. Drain, refresh, and peel. Cut the tomatoes in half, remove the seeds and coarsely chop the flesh.

Melt 3 tablespoons butter, add the remaining chopped shallot and cook until translucent. Add the chopped tomato, bay leaf, tomato paste, and a pinch of sugar. Season to taste and simmer 20 minutes, stirring often. Remove from heat and cool at room temperature.

Preheat oven to 350°F (180°C).

Bone the cooked frogs' legs and set aside.

Butter 8 ramekins. Use a pastry bag to spread a little mousse over the bottom and sides of the ramekins. Leave a hollow in the middle.

Fill the hollow with the frogs'-leg meat and cover with second layer of mousse. Place the ramekins in a pan of hot water and bake for 15 minutes. Bind the cooking liquid from the frogs' legs with the teaspoon of roux and boil. Add the rest of the crème fraîche and whisk over low heat, without boiling, while adding 5 tablespoons of butter cut into cubes. Add the lemon juice, correct the seasoning.

Place mounds of spinach on serving plates. Unmold the contents of the ramekins and place one of the mousseline disks on each mound of spinach. Top with the sauce and garnish with a little tomato purée. Sprinkle with chopped chives.

SERVES 6

For the frogs' legs and frogs'-leg mousse
• 4 lb frogs' legs
• 5 shallots chopped
• 2 tablespoons butter
• ½ bottle Riesling
• ½ lb flaked pike
• 2 egg whites
• 2 cups crème fraîche (part to be used for the mousse and part to finish)

For the spinach
• 1 lb fresh spinach
• 1 unpeeled garlic clove
• 3 tablespoons butter

For the tomato purée
• 2 tomatoes
• 3 tablespoons butter
• 1 shallot chopped
• 1 pinch sugar
• 1 bay leaf
• 2 teaspoons tomato paste
• Salt, pepper

• 1 teaspoon roux (half and half melted butter and flour)
• 5 tablespoons butter
• ½ lemon
• ½ bunch chives, chopped

PREPARATION TIME
45 minutes

COOKING TIME
30 minutes

The art of pastry-making.

SERVES 4
• 4 slices fillet of char weighing about 4 oz each
• 2 lb potatoes ("ratte" variety)
• 1 cup heavy cream
• Nutmeg
• Ground Espelette red pepper
• 3 tablespoons hazelnut oil
• 3 tablespoons butter
• 4 tablespoons Sevruga caviar
• Salt, pepper

PREPARATION TIME
45 minutes

COOKING TIME
30 minutes

Char with Iranian Caviar, Mousseline of Potatoes with Hazelnut Oil

Cook the whole unpeeled potatoes in a pot of boiling salted water. Drain, and peel while still hot. Put the potatoes through a food mill and return to pot.

Scald the heavy cream with a pinch of grated nutmeg and ground Espelette red pepper. Add to the potatoes and stir vigorously with a wooden spatula. Correct the seasoning and add the hazelnut oil. Place the pot of mousseline potatoes in a pan of hot water and keep warm.

Heat 3 tablespoons butter in a frying pan until foamy, add the char fillets and sauté on both sides until the flesh turns pink.

Heap mounds of mousseline potatoes on serving plates, top with a char fillet, and garnish with a spoonful of caviar. Serve.

SERVES 8
• 1 lobe fresh goose foie gras (about 2 lb)
• ½ tablespoon salt
• ⅛ cup cognac
• ⅛ cup port wine
• 1½ oz fresh truffle, peeled and chopped
• 6 tablespoons goose fat

PREPARATION TIME
35 minutes (beginning 24 hours in advance)

COOKING TIME
40 minutes

Goose Liver Terrine with Truffles

24 HOURS IN ADVANCE
Use a paring knife to cut the foie gras in two and carefully remove the veins and nerves.

Season with the salt, cognac, and port. Allow to macerate for 24 hours.

Preheat oven to 210°F (100°C).

Place the foie gras in an earthenware or porcelain terrine. Press gently to spread evenly.

Make a small opening with the finger, insert the chopped truffle, press the opening closed again. Cover the terrine.

Place the terrine in a pan of hot water and bake for 45 minutes.

Allow the terrine to cool in the pan of hot water. Remove the lid and cover the cooked foie gras with melted goose fat. Cool. Serve with a spoon dipped in hot water.

This terrine can be stored for two weeks in the refrigerator.

SERVES 8
- 1 tablespoon yeast
- ½ cup milk, warmed
- 2 cups flour
- 1 teaspoon salt
- ½ cup sugar
- 3 eggs
- 1 cup softened butter &
  3 tablespoons butter for
  greasing the pan
- 4 oz Malaga raisins softened
  in 1 tablespoon kirsch
- 10 whole almonds
- 1 tablespoon
  confectioners' sugar

PREPARATION TIME
35 minutes & 1 hour 30
minutes for rising

COOKING TIME
1 hour

*Eleven o'clock—time for a break
before serving lunch.*

Gugelhopf

Dissolve the yeast in half of the warm milk, add 2 tablespoons flour, knead 5 minutes and allow to rise for about 10 minutes in a warm spot.

When the yeast starter has risen somewhat, add the rest of the flour, the salt, sugar, and remaining warm milk. Stir. Add the eggs and half of the softened butter. Beat the dough vigorously while gradually adding the rest of the butter. When the dough pulls away from the sides of the bowl, work in the raisins and the kirsch. Cover with a damp cloth and allow to rise in a warm spot for 1 hour 30 minutes.

Preheat oven to 350°F (180°C).

When the dough has doubled in bulk, knock it down with the fist and roll into a ball. Butter a gugelhopf mold (a fluted ring mold) and press a whole almond into each indentation of the fluting. Place the ball of dough in the mold, pushing it evenly against the sides. Bake for 1 hour.

When the gugelhopf is cooked, turn it upside-down and remove from pan, cool, and dredge with confectioners' sugar.

Glazed Rose Petals to Accompany a Glass of Gewürtraminer

MAKES 12 PETALS
- 12 pink rose petals from unsprayed blooms
- 1 egg white
- 4 teaspoons sugar

PREPARATION TIME
5 minutes

COOKING TIME
4 hours

Carefully rinse the rose petals under a stream of cold water and dry separately on a sheet of absorbent paper.

Preheat oven to minimum (about 85°F [30°C]).

In a bowl, beat the egg white until foamy. Dip a pastry brush in the beaten egg white and carefully coat each rose petal. Cover a baking sheet with ovenproof paper and arrange the rose petals on it, making sure they do not touch. Sprinkle each petal with sugar.

Bake the petals for 4 hours, or until the sugar is hard and crystallized. If necessary, open the oven door occasionally in order cool the interior and maintain the lowest possible temperature.

Serve the glazed rose petals as a novel accompaniment to a glass of Gewürztraminer.

Peaches Haeberlin

SERVES 4
- 4 white peaches
- 1 cup water
- 1 cup sugar
- 1 vanilla pod
- 8 egg yolks
- ½ bottle Champagne
- 4 scoops pistachio ice cream
- ½ cup heavy cream, whipped

PREPARATION TIME
30 minutes

COOKING TIME
40 minutes

Stem the peaches and immerse in a pot of boiling water for 1 minute. Refresh and peel carefully.

Combine 1 cup water and 1 cup sugar in a pot. Add the vanilla pod, split and scraped, and boil for 10 minutes. Poach the whole peaches, with their pits, for 5 minutes in the sugar syrup. Drain and cool at room temperature. Note that poached peaches may be prepared in bulk during the season, placed in sterilized jars with the vanilla syrup, and closed hermetically for storage.

Ten minutes before serving, make the Sabayon cream. Place the egg yolks in the top half of a double boiler, beat until lemon colored, stir in the Champagne. Fill the bottom half of the double boiler with water, bring to the boil, then reduce to a simmer. Place the top half of the double boiler over the simmering water and whisk the egg mixture until it thickens. Remove from heat and continue whisking until the mixture cools.

Place a poached peach in the middle of a large soup plate, cover with Sabayon cream, and serve with a scoop of pistachio ice cream garnished with the whipped cream.

NICOLAS LE BEC

LES LOGES

LYON

THE MAN

A year here, a month there, a stint in Paris, another in New York, back to the Paris area and then down to a luxury hotel on the Riviera…it's easy to lose track of Nicolas le Bec's early travels. But, as he explains, in those days he was only eighteen, twenty, twenty-two years old. He was at an age when he was eager to try everything, watch the world's greatest chefs at work, learn ten recipes for puff pastry so he could invent his own, absorb everything on the quiet before giving his notice. He learned his lessons and won his freedom.

He had the right background for it. Le Bec began cooking at the age of thirteen, and remembers playing with the tin pie-plates in the kitchen as a tiny child. Today, at the tender age of thirty, he's already an old campaigner. He says Lyon is the end of the line. Then he thinks again. No, he still has a way to go.

Perhaps, but today Le Bec reigns over a very fine kingdom indeed. His playground is Les Loges, four Renaissance houses built around a central courtyard, a patio, and the paving-stones of the Saint-Jean quarter of Lyon. The restaurant is tucked into a corner of the patio below the hotel. Just a few tables, which are reserved for initiates and unnoticed by other passers-by. At nightfall the lacquered wooden tables are covered with gray tablecloths. Servers dressed in charcoal gray glide gracefully back and forth under the glass skylight. Strategically placed lights gleam under the natural-stone arcades surrounding the patio. It is as elegant and understated as a New York hotel with a French designer's touch.

This one, however, belongs to the very French chain Les Hôtels de Montagne, which also owns several establishments in Megève and a luxury hotel in the Lubéron. Le Bec has spent the past seven years working for this upmarket family business. He personally supervised the installation of the kitchens in each new acquisition, which in practice involved commuting between the various hotels in the chain. This proved an exhausting marathon.

"Behind the wheel of my ancient Audi, I sometimes clocked up 40,000 miles in six months"

Things at Les Loges are different. Since owner Jean-Louis Sibuet offered Le Bec a partnership, he's on his own turf here. The downside is that he's not as free as before. He's no longer able to take off whenever he wants.

He makes up for it in his cuisine. Since his arrival, all his adventures have been culinary, revolutionizing the hackneyed flavors that are familiar in this city, which has a reputation for conventional bourgeois tastes. Dressed in dark colors, like the rest of his staff, youthful and outspoken, he's seen—mistakenly, he insists—as anti-Bocuse. He attracted notice from the media, and also from food critics. In 2002, or fourteen months after his arrival at Les Loges, Nicolas Le Bec was named chef of the year by Gault et Millaut. However, he still hasn't made a dent in the Michelin Guide. Well, at least that gives the media something to talk about.

Strategic decision-making.

Facing page:
A dining room in the Les Loges restaurant.

Nicolas Le Bec represents the new generation of chefs, a generation that are often skillful communicators. He conceives cuisine as a global concept. He believes it is not just a matter of knowing how to make a sauce base, but also how to write a menu using just the right words, how to enhance a dish with a jot of the pencil, how to design memorable plates. Nicolas recently opened his own bistro, a little gem in which close attention is given to the smallest detail. Glass globes in the foyer. Grilled fish and meat ordered by weight. Mashed potatoes and a fricassee of chanterelle mushrooms as the universal garnish. This concept facilitates service, maintains individual product quality, and projects a modern slant.

But Nicolas Le Bec leaves nothing to chance. He's behind his stove every night, actively improvising and constantly modifying his own recipes. He eats little, sleeps little. A man of paradox, he claims he never has time to taste one of his finished dishes. The important thing is inventing them.

THE REGION

He's stubborn, this Breton. He maintains that no, Lyon's products are not the best in the world. He doesn't buy his fish at the city's central market, he doesn't buy his Saint-Marcellin cheese from La Mère Richard. About the only local specialty to have won his favor is Colette Sibilia's pistachio sausage. He still uses his regular suppliers for everything else. This makes waves in France's gastronomic capital, but he's used to making waves.

The fact is, that in order to enlarge Les Fermes de Marie at Megève and supply the string of restaurants that followed, he had to fight for favorable contracts. "When I first arrived in Megève, you couldn't find a single fresh vegetable in the whole town. Trucks didn't want to make the climb." But now, just a few years later, tons of fresh products are delivered to his kitchens by truck every day. This creates relationships. At Lyon, Le Bec simply drew on his personal network as the only sensible way to do business. This means you won't find quenelles with Nantua sauce or poached chicken at Les Loges. Even good old Charolais beef is gradually giving way to Bavarian veal. Jerusalem artichokes, rhubarb, celery (root and branch), are a few of Le Bec's favorite vegetables. Just for the fun of freeing them from oblivion? No. Because they're good winter vegetables. When it comes to seasonings, he shamelessly adds a few pinches of Chinese spice to the aromatic herbs of Provence and Savoy. In general he prefers fresh herbs to stale powders, but he doesn't rule anything out. He's as happy cooking breast of Sologne duck as he is boiling Brittany lobster or roasting an Alba truffle. His aim is to be free, as free as the times we live in.

THE STYLE

Le Bec changes his menu every month, but the underlying principle remains the same. "Green zucchini peel with eucalyptus, steamed fillet of cod, tender grilled squid." Or, "purple artichokes with tarragon sprouts, breast of squab demi-sel in cedar wood." Vegetables are the star attraction, a policy that's obvious from the beginning to the end of every meal. When ordering from the menu, guests try to read between the lines in order to visualize what's coming. They do so in vain. Only Le Bec knows.

Nicolas Le Bec is no vegetarian, but he puts ingredients in their proper place and establishes new hierarchies. The frontier separating the dish from its garnish has been abolished. The plate presents a whole. This is true even for the desserts, which raise the ante by being arranged around a simple single pear, mango, or cocoa bean.

Facing page:
Nicolas Le Bec's realm, under the arcades of the venerable courtyard at Les Loges.

Left to right:
Service at the Les Loges café. Aromatic oils. The full range is on sale at the Café Épicerie. Table-setting at the Les Loges restaurant.

A busy morning before lunch:
pots simmer on the stove.

Facing page:
Entrance to the Café Épicerie.

Stylistic eccentricity? Not solely. "I like vegetables, for their flavor, their color, and their texture. They're inexpensive ingredients that provide a good base for creativity. In any case, when I arrived in Lyon after Savoy, I wanted to invent a light, urban cuisine."

Nicolas Le Bec doesn't like to stand still. And he's the first to recognize that there are fashions in cuisine—while also refusing to admit any direct influence from his peers. "It's our customers who demand changes. Changes reflecting their lifestyles, their concerns of the moment, the trips they've taken. It's up to us to keep up with them, to invent new dishes based on consumer aspirations." Le Bec adapts. At Megève, his guests spend their whole holiday on skis. In Provence, they spend it loafing in the sun. In Lyon, they're taking a short break from busy, sedentary, urban lives. Different contexts call for different styles of cuisine. In Lyon, Nicolas' cuisine is streamlined. It goes with the décor, the plates, and the servers' smiles. Unity of form and content.

SERVES 4
- 4 medium-sized raw mackerel
- 2 cups white wine
- 2 cups distilled vinegar
- 1 medium green pepper, chopped
- 2 teaspoons dried coriander
- 3 tablespoons fresh ginger, grated
- 2 carrots
- 2 ribs celery, pared and chopped
- 2 bay leaves
- 1 tablespoon sugar
- Salt, pepper

PREPARATION TIME
30 minutes

COOKING TIME
20 minutes

Maintaining high standards.

Marinated Mackerel as Served at the Café Epicerie

Cut the fillets from the mackerel, remove the bones, and rinse one-by-one under a stream of cold water. Dry in a cloth and arrange in pairs in the bottom half of small, lidded, glass serving dishes.

For the marinade, mix together the white wine, vinegar, green pepper, coriander, ginger, carrots, celery and bay leaves in a pot. Add 1 tablespoon sugar. Season to taste and simmer 20 minutes.

Cover the mackerel in the glass serving dishes with equal parts of the marinade. Adjust the lids, cool at room temperature, then chill in the refrigerator.

Serve the mackerel fillets very cold with a little of the marinade.

SERVES 4

For the celery cream
- 1 celery root
- 1 cup water
- 1 cup milk
- 1 tablespoon sea salt
- 2 tablespoons grated horseradish
- 1 cup heavy cream
- Salt, pepper

For the oysters and cucumber aspic
- 12 large Brittany oysters
- 1 cucumber
- 2 sheets gelatin

To garnish
- A few watercress leaves
- Lemon-flavored olive oil
- A dab of tarama

PREPARATION TIME
45 minutes

STANDING TIME
2 hours

COOKING TIME
30 minutes

The Black Angel in a cloud of steam.

Celery Cream with Horseradish, Large Brittany Oysters, Cucumber Aspic, Fresh Watercress, and Tarama

• *Preparing the celery cream*: Peel the celery root, cut into cubes, and simmer in equal parts water and milk seasoned with 1 tablespoon sea salt for 30 minutes.

Drain, cool, and mix in blender with the grated horseradish. Whip the cream and add to the celery and horseradish mixture. Season to taste and set aside in a cool spot.

• *Preparing the oysters and cucumber aspic*: Open 12 oysters, carefully remove from shell and drain on a cloth. Pour off the juices in the shell and set aside. Soften the gelatin in a little cold water.

Put the cucumber through the blender, add the oyster-shell juices and the softened gelatin. Blend until the gelatin is dissolved. Press through a fine strainer. Discard the cucumber pulp, retaining only the clear juice. Refrigerate for 2 hours.

Place a small mound of celery cream on each plate. Top with the raw oysters and a tablespoon of cucumber aspic. Garnish with a few watercress leaves dressed with lemon-flavored olive oil. Decorate with a dab of tarama. Serve immediately.

SERVES 4
- 4 oz string beans
- 4 Brittany lobsters weighing about 1 lb each
- 1 carrot, peeled and chopped
- 1 onion, peeled and chopped
- 1 head garlic, peeled and chopped
- ⅓ cup port wine
- ⅓ cup cognac
- 1 tablespoon tomato paste
- 2 bay leaves
- 5 juniper berries
- ½ celery root (center portion), peeled and cut into 4 very thin slices
- Leaves from ½ sprig basil, washed and chopped & 1 whole sprig for decoration
- 3 tablespoons butter
- Salt, pepper

PREPARATION TIME
50 minutes

COOKING TIME
30 minutes

A minimalist slant.

Celery Root and Steamed Brittany-Lobster Ravioli with Fresh Basil

Cook the string beans in a pot of boiling salted water until done. Refresh in ice water.

Drain and cut into small even pieces.

Immerse the lobsters for 10 seconds in a large pot of generously salted water and refresh immediately in a bowl of ice water.

Remove the lobster meat from the tail and claws. Set aside the shells from the heads for decoration, crush the rest and transfer to a large pot. Add the carrot, onion, garlic, port wine, cognac, tomato paste, bay leaves, and juniper berries. Cover with cold water, bring to a boil, reduce heat, and simmer 30 minutes.

Strain the broth into a clean pot, return to heat, reduce to three-quarters of its volume, and set aside in a warm spot.

Cook the celery-root slices for 1 minute in boiling salted water, refresh in ice water.

Cut the lobster meat into small pieces and combine in a bowl with the string beans and chopped basil leaves. Season to taste. Place a portion of the lobster mixture on each slice of celery root. Bring the edges of the celery-root slices up and over the lobster mixture. Wrap in plastic film and squeeze in order to form small, ravioli-like balls.

Just before serving time, steam the lobster-ravioli balls for 10 minutes.

Bring the sauce to a simmer, add the butter, and whip until blended. Season to taste and pour over the lobster ravioli.

Garnish the ravioli with the leaves from the remaining sprig of basil and the lobster-head shells trimmed with kitchen shears.

Serve very hot.

Filled Zucchini Blossoms and Steamed Medallions of Turbot with Provençal Herb Sauce

• *Preparing the zucchini*: Wash the zucchini and cut into thick slices without removing the skin. Season to taste and sprinkle with 3 tablespoons olive oil. Steam the slices for 20 minutes, drain, and press in a cloth to remove excess moisture.

In a bowl, combine the zucchini slices with the egg plus the 2 egg yolks and the garlic. Season to taste, add 3 tablespoons olive oil. Blend in a food processor. Fill the zucchini blossoms with this mixture and set aside at room temperature.

• *Preparing the provençal herb sauce*: Place the mussels in a large pot with the shallot, white wine, and bouquet garni. Cover and cook over high heat for about 10 minutes, shaking occasionally, until the mussels open.

Strain the pot juices into a saucepan, add the fish stock and simmer 5 minutes over low heat. Remove from heat and add the aromatic herbs to the boiling liquid.

Cover with plastic film and allow to steep for 10 minutes. Remove the herbs, set the stock aside and keep warm.

Steam the stuffed zucchini blossoms for 20 minutes. Poach the slices of turbot for 10 minutes in simmering salted water and drain on a dry cloth.

Arrange the slices of turbot and the stuffed zucchini blossoms on individual plates. Bring the Provençal herb sauce to a boil, add 3 tablespoons olive oil and the butter.

Whip with a wire whisk until thoroughly blended. Season to taste and pour over the fish. Serve immediately.

SERVES 4
- 3 lb turbot cut into 4 even slices
- 8 small zucchini
- 4 zucchini blossoms
- 6 tablespoons olive oil
- 1 egg & 2 yolks
- ½ clove garlic, peeled and chopped
- Salt, pepper

For the provençal herb sauce
- 1 lb mussels
- 1 shallot, peeled and chopped
- ¼ cup white wine
- Bouquet garni
- ⅓ cup fish stock
- 1 sprig fresh thyme
- 1 sprig sage
- 1 rib fennel
- 1 sprig rosemary
- 3 tablespoons extra-virgin olive oil
- 3 tablespoons butter
- Salt, pepper

PREPARATION TIME
45 minutes

COOKING TIME
45 minutes

Turning up the heat.

SERVES 4
- 4 pink grapefruit, plus 5 extra for juice (9 in total)
- ½ bunch fresh verbena & 1 sprig for decoration
- ¾ cup sugar
- 1 vanilla pod
- 5 tablespoons apple pectin
- 2 very ripe mangoes
- 5 lumps sugar
- 2 tablespoons water
- 12 shelled dried hazelnuts

PREPARATION TIME
1 hour 30 minutes

COOKING TIME
25 minutes

In the courtyard of Les Loges, one of the architectural gems of the Saint Jean quarter.

Fresh Sliced Mango and Pink-Grapefruit Segments Glazed with a Sauce of Verbena and Passion Fruit

Squeeze the five extra grapefruit. There should be 2 cups of juice. In a saucepan, heat the juice to lukewarm. Add the verbena, cover with plastic film and allow to steep for 45 minutes.

Strain this liquid into another pot. Add the sugar, and the vanilla pod split in two. Bring to the boil and add the apple pectin, which will thicken the liquid. Set aside at room temperature.

Pare the remaining grapefruit, use a sharp knife to remove the sections, and set aside in a cool spot. Peel the mangoes and cut into slices about 1/5-inch thick.

Combine the lumps of sugar with 2 tablespoons water and heat, stirring, until the mixture caramelizes. When the caramel is golden, remove from heat and add the hazelnuts, stirring to coat each kernel thoroughly.

Place a mound of fresh fruit on each plate, alternating the mango slices with the grapefruit segments.

Cover with the verbena syrup.

Garnish with the fresh verbena leaves and caramel-coated hazelnuts.

MARC MENEAU

L'ESPÉRANCE

SAINT-PÈRE SOUS VÉZELAY

THE MAN

Marc Meneau wears a tie under his white chef's coat, a subtle reminder of the exalted status he enjoys in the village where his double-M monogram is regally inscribed on the gates of his estate. Behind the gates lie a lush sculpture garden, a small canal, and a series of wooden bridges. The interior of the house boasts wall tapestries, displays of pewter-ware, a library, and bottle-green marble columns. The glass skylight over the dining room, our host points out proudly, was installed before the architects of Paris's Forum des Halles had the same idea, implying that the original concept was his.

The house has been redecorated three times. With each new incarnation, Marc Meneau measures the distance he's traveled from the adjacent café-grocery run by his parents. He learned everything he knows on his own. Yes, he trained at a hotel school, but in the management department, where cookery was not taught. He learned how to cook himself, from books—dozens of books: read, reread, memorized. "I won my first star with recipes copied out of books. When you're untrained, you can't make mistakes. You have to do your marketing with all the personal commitment of a housewife shopping for her family." Three neighbors, all of them famous chefs, all now retired, helped him along the way. It was like having teachers right at home with him. He eventually struck out on his own, but never forgot what they taught him. Today he still reads a lot, and even owns a unique collection of rare books. But because he's inventive, he's now more of a writer than a reader.

He writes about everything: cooking and famous historical figures; cooking and painting; cooking and film. And on every kind of relationship between cooking and the other arts. He's broadened his horizons, and has now become a sort of scholarly archive. He served as technical adviser to the actor Gérard Depardieu for the role of Vatel, who was in charge of cooking for the Duc de Condé in the seventeenth century. He's the acknowledged king of historical reproduction, and has duplicated the banquet of the Heptameron (from the classic collection of old French tales) and the state dinner of Yalta for his friends. He simplifies things, of course, reproducing the spirit rather than the letter of the past event. He's recently become interested in Cistercian cuisine. "I needed to know more about religion. When you grow up in Vézelay, you're naturally intrigued by religion. And I discovered that the monks were actually the first to do almost everything."

And then there's his professional career. Earning and losing a third star in the Michelin Guide. Entertaining the musician Serge Gainsbourg and the Russian cellist and composer Rostropovich for several months at his hotel. Entertaining fans of his cuisine, who make the round-trip from Paris by helicopter. A new, very "jet-set" restaurant planned for Gstadt. But always, no matter what he does, the Eternal Hillside of Vézelay is his beacon. "It's a site of great spiritual purity, of fresh starts. People have been coming here since the time of ancient Gaul in search of strength for the battles to come. It's a place that sustains my fundamental philosophy, which is to continue inventing new recipes forever."

THE REGION

His favorite products? Everything good. Not necessarily things that come from Burgundy. He laughingly dismisses snails as no better than offal, and was happy to leave frogs' legs—even those from Les Dombes—to his late neighbor Loiseau. Meneau would rather drink wine than pour it into sauces. "We're no longer living in the horse-and-buggy era. Today products from the ends of the earth can be delivered to us in twelve hours. My region is the whole world." Result: if strawberries from Chili are good in December, why not serve them? If vegetable fritters made with rice flour are lighter, use rice flour. Purists can always call it tempura if that makes them feel any better.

And yet, this man is a true Burgundian. His family has lived in Saint-Père for five centuries, and the archives prove it. In his lifetime his work has moved only seventy-five feet, from his parents' café to the inn he oversees today. He knows his village like the back of his hand, runs into cousins all the time, and feels vaguely guilty for

Left to right:
Marc Meneau has taken a
personal interest in the
Bourgogne-Vézelay vintage.
Freshly harvested walnuts.
A caviar duo:
mousse plus fritter.

The Burgundy pasturelands.

Page 122:
One of the notebooks Marc Meneau uses to jot down his impressions—often in the form of recipes—when he travels.

Page 123:
The chef bids goodbye to departing guests.

having betrayed his roots by purchasing a house a mile away, near the Vézelay Basilica. "There'll always be rivalry between two villages. And the Church of Saint-Pierre, a flamboyant Gothic monument, was built to compete with the Marie-Madeleine Basilica."

By way of atonement, Marc Meneau has worked with friends from Saint-Pierre to restore the luster of Vézelay wine. The vineyard on these Morvan slopes had virtually disappeared. Meneau acquired a plot of his own and used his fame to promote the revived Bourgogne-Vézelay vintage. "I needed to put down roots again and renew my contact with the land."

Meneau is proud of his Burgundian heritage, but he expresses it through his overall spirit rather than through the specific ingredients used in his kitchen. His cuisine features uncomplicated sensations and flavors; balanced textures. When a dish of scallops is carried past us, he explains: "Now there's a real Burgundian dish." They lie in a crisp pastry shell. Nothing could be simpler. It is just a "bite to eat," in every sense of the term, like a ploughman's lunch. Under the shellfish is a slice of beef marrow. Beef is important. A real local product if ever there was one, although the legendary Charolais steers are raised farther south. Yes, but what about those scallops? "You don't think scallops are local? Take a look around. Scallop shells everywhere. They symbolize Saint James and are carried atop the staffs of pilgrims making their way to Compostela."

THE STYLE

Marc Meneau believes in the power of the written word. Whenever he leaves Saint-Père, he always takes his notebooks with him. He jots down everything. A quotation from Jean-Jacques Rousseau, an aphorism, an unusual word, a recipe that's stuck in

BEURRE DE ...

J'utilise ce beurre
qui est un des meilleurs
du monde.

Dane Joveau

PAMPLIE

laiterie   DEUX-SÈVRES   coopérative

his mind like one of those melodies you can't get out of your head. He has quite a pile of notebooks now, more than two hundred. Sometimes he goes back to earlier ones and finds a recipe that didn't seem practical at the time. But tastes have changed. Maybe now is the time to try it out. This is one way Marc Meneau keeps his revolution going.

When creating something new, he works freely around a few basic principles. One of these guiding principles is the combination, on a single plate, of a simple preparation with a sophisticated one. An example is the caviar cream, currently served in two silver spoons—one warm, the other cold. The cold spoon is piled with caviar cream; the warm spoon holds a crisp mashed-potato cake filled with the same luxurious cream—country fare meets urban sophistication.

Another principle is to combine products from the same region. Beans with foie gras, truffles with olive oil, angler with rice grown in the water where the fish was caught. An illustration of this "world-according-to-Meneau" is his intriguing combination of scallops with wilted sugar-beet greens. "It's Le Touquet on a plate: beet fields meeting the sea." Another: beef-tartare cannelloni with oysters. This time the allusion is to Normandy, where cows graze beside oyster beds. Meanwhile, of course, Meneau also presents the classic repertoire of French cuisine. He has nothing against flans, béarnaise sauce, shellfish butter, or soufflés. But he prepares these classics in his own way, creating unusual combinations and experimenting with different effects. He might braid a crown of meringue around truffle cream, or split a carrot, stuff it with cumin and foie gras, and reconstruct it. A super carrot with stuffing. Or he might have the maître d'hôtel remove a square slice from the top of a brioche to reveal the superb flesh of turbot inside. As a grand finale, the pineapple arrives studded with vanilla beans. Dining at Meneau's is baroque theater.

Facing page and above:
Marc Meneau is happy to promote fine French produce.

SERVES 4
- 8 clams
- ½ lb sea salt
- 8 strips aluminum foil (¾ × 6 inches [2 × 15 cm])
- ¾ cup olive oil
- ½ cup smoked olive oil (available at specialty grocery shops)
- Salt, pepper

PREPARATION TIME
10 minutes, plus overnight soaking

COOKING TIME
35 minutes

Clams Baked in Embers with Smoked Olive Oil

- *The night before*: Place the clams in a bowl of water and sea salt. Cover and refrigerate overnight.

Drain the clams and rinse well in fresh water. Wrap the clams in the aluminum-foil strips, place under a pile of glowing embers and bake for 10 minutes. Remove from the embers, unwrap, and open slightly. Pour ½ teaspoon smoked oil into each clam and season with salt and pepper. Arrange the clams on a bed of sea salt and serve very hot.

SERVES 2
- ¾ lb cod with the skin
- Coarse salt, pepper
- 2 egg yolks
- ½ lb leaf spinach
- A few candied lemon rinds

For the salt crust
- 1 cup flour
- 6 tablespoons coarse salt
- 1 tablespoon regular salt
- Blossoms from 1 sprig of thyme
- 1 egg white
- 6 tablespoons water

For the lobster butter
- ½ lb European-lobster shells (claws and body)
- 8 oz softened unsalted butter

For the lightly salted butter
- 4 oz unsalted butter
- 2 teaspoons crushed Guérande salt

PREPARATION TIME
1 hour

COOKING TIME
40 minutes

Cod in Salt Crust

- *Preparing the salt crust*: Mix together the flour, coarse salt, regular salt, thyme blossoms, egg white, and water. Form this paste into a ball, dredge lightly with flour, cover with plastic film, and chill.
- *Preparing the lobster butter*: Crush the lobster shells with an electric beater. Add 8 oz of the softened butter and beat at low speed for about 15 minutes (this process can be done by hand, using a wooden spatula). Transfer the butter mixture to a saucepan, place the saucepan next to a burner on low, and barely simmer for about 1 hour. At the end of this period, pour the butter into a strainer lined with a clean cloth. Strain and chill.
- *Preparing the lightly salted butter*: Mix the remaining 4 oz of butter with the crushed Guérande salt. Using a ridged wooden spoon designed for the purpose, form the salted butter into shells. Chill.
- *Preparing the cod*: Preheat the oven to 460°F (240°C). Place 6 tablespoons of the lobster butter in the bottom of an aluminum-foil container large enough to accommodate the piece of cod. Rub the cod on both sides with pepper and coarse salt. Place it on top of the lobster butter. Roll out the ball of salt paste as thinly as possible and wrap it around the aluminum-foil container, covering the cod completely. Glaze with the beaten egg yolks and bake for 12 minutes. When the salt crust is fully browned, the cod is cooked. Set aside and keep warm for about 10 minutes.

Just before serving, reheat the cod for a few moments in the hot oven. Transfer to a serving plate, leaving the salt crust intact, and cover with a large napkin. Serve the butter shells separately. Accompany with mounds of spinach wilted in butter and garnished with candied lemon peel.

SERVES 4
For the vegetable broth
• 1 onion
• 2 ribs celery
• 1 leek
• 7 tablespoons olive oil
• Chicken stock, clarified
• 2 potatoes
• 1 carrot
• 1 turnip
• 1 zucchini
• ½ lb peas
• 4 oz string beans
• 1 cup chickpeas

For the beef ravioli
• 4 oz fillet of beef
• 4 oysters
• 1 shallot
• ¼ cup black olives
• Ready-to-cook ravioli dough
• ½ truffle
• 2 oz Parmesan cheese
• 1 cup fresh almonds, shredded
• 4 oz vermicelli
• Sprig of lovage
• Salt, pepper, Tabasco sauce

PREPARATION TIME
1 hour

COOKING TIME
1 hour

Beef Ravioli with a Vegetable Broth

• *Preparing the vegetable broth*: Cook the onion, celery, and leek until translucent in 4 tablespoons of the olive oil. Season to taste, add the chicken stock, heat to boiling. Chop the potatoes, carrot, and turnip, add to the stock, and reduce heat to a simmer.

Cook the zucchini briefly in 2 tablespoons olive oil. Shell the peas, chop the string beans, and steam until tender. When the vegetables in the stock are done, add the zucchini, peas, and string beans. Cook the chickpeas in boiling salted water until tender.

• *Preparing the beef ravioli*: Using a knife, shred the beef and the oysters. Combine. Peel and chop the shallot, cook in 1 tablespoon olive oil until golden. Shred the olives. Add the shallot and olives to the beef mixture. Season with salt, pepper, and a few drops of Tabasco sauce. Cut out 4 large squares of ravioli dough, poach in boiling salted water until tender but firm. Drain the cooked squares, spread on a flat surface, fill with the stuffing, and roll into cylinders, tucking in the ends.

On each of four large soup plates, place one stuffed ravioli. Surround with the chickpeas and other vegetables.

Fill the plates halfway with the vegetable broth.

Garnish the stuffed ravioli with a slice of truffle, a sliver of Parmesan cheese, the almonds, vermicelli, and the lovage leaves.

Shelling walnuts.

SERVES 2
- 2 slices white bread
  ⅓ inch thick
- Butter
- Sea-urchin flesh
- 1 marrow
- 4 large scallops
- Fleur de sel
- Freshly ground pepper
- Whipped butter

PREPARATION TIME
30 minutes

COOKING TIME
20 minutes

*Preparation of fish using scissors
and tweezers is an exacting task.*

Scallop Canapés with Marrow

Sauté the bread in butter. Purée the sea-urchin flesh. Soak the marrow in cold water for 1 hour, then poach in salted water.

Remove the scallops from their shells, rinse, and drain on a cloth. Grill the scallops just long enough to mark them.

Spread the sautéed bread with the sea-urchin purée.

Cut the marrow into thin, ⅓ inch (½ cm) slices.

Season the scallops with fleur de sel and freshly ground pepper, place on top of the marrow. Decorate the edge of the plate with a ribbon of whipped butter.

SERVES 2
- 8 ripe fragrant strawberries (gariguette variety, for example)
- Balsamic vinegar
- Sugar syrup cooked to 320°F
- Ground Sechuan pepper
- Ground angelica seeds
- Ground cubeb pepper
- Chopped fresh peppermint
- Japanese pearl tapioca
- Coconut milk

For the Sechuan sauce
- 3 cups white port wine
- 2 teaspoons pectin
- 3 tablespoons sugar
- 1 teaspoon freshly ground Sechuan pepper

For the angelica sauce
- 4 cups cream
- 12 angelica seeds ground with a pestle in a mortar
- 2 tablespoons sugar
- 2 tablespoons lemon juice

For the cubeb-pepper sauce
- 3 cups ruby port
- 2 teaspoons pectin
- 3 tablespoons sugar
- 1 tablespoon freshly ground cubeb pepper
- 8 juniper berries

For the peppermint sauce
- 4 cups cream
- 6 tablespoons fresh peppermint, chopped
- 2 tablespoons sugar

PREPARATION TIME
40 minutes

COOKING TIME
30 minutes

The fireplace in the library-salon is also used for preparing grilled meat.

Peppery Spiced Strawberries

Prepare the sauces by combining the ingredients for each one and simmering until reduced by one-half. The sauces should be smooth and syrupy. Set aside.

Dip 4 strawberries in balsamic vinegar and arrange in a straight line on a large plate. Dip the other 4 strawberries in the sugar syrup and arrange in a line parallel with the first one. Place a small mound of each ground spice next to each of the sugar-syrup-coated strawberries. Pour a little of the corresponding sauce next to each mound of powdered spice.

Serve the remainder of all the sauces separately.

For color and texture contrast, garnish the plate with Japanese pearl tapioca cooked in coconut milk. If Japanese pearl tapioca is not available, a scoop of good vanilla ice cream can provide the desired contrast.

The strawberries should be prepared and served at room temperature.

ALAIN PASSARD

L'ARPÈGE

PARIS

THE MAN

Alain Passard is proud of his restaurant's stylish décor, its Lalique glass and light wood paneling. But his pride and joy is his kitchen: he wouldn't trade that for anything in the world. It suits him. It's small—so small, in fact, that his staff have to watch every move they make. In Passard's words, "It's like an haute-couture workshop. A closed environment in which each skilled craftsman has a specific role and each gives their best to create masterpieces of finesse."

Passard speaks from experience. His father was a musician, but his mother was a couturiere. He would have been happy to work with her, but in the depths of rural Brittany that just wasn't done. So, at the age of fourteen, he decided to become a chef, which is the only other career that's both a trade and an art. He saw an ad in the local newspaper, "Seeking apprentice chef," and answered it. Meanwhile, he also earned his CAP (professional aptitude certificate) by correspondence. Fate took care of the rest: a stint at the Hôtellerie du Lion d'Or working under a two-star chef, followed by an apprenticeship in Reims with the Boyer family's father-and-son team. Next came the crucial meeting with Alain Senderens at his restaurant—at the time called L'Archestrate—on the Rue de Varenne in Paris. In 1986, after brief interlude at the Duc d'Enghien, Passard returned to L'Archestrate and renamed it L'Arpège. His kingdom.

He's been at his post between the Assemblée Nationale and the Rodin Museum, with the dome of the Invalides in the background, for fifteen years now. That's about long it takes to become a real Parisian, and Passard now is one. "This city has a lighthearted, carefree spirit that I think I'd have a hard time finding in the provinces. Guests at Passard's restaurant greet each other, mingle, pass comments from table to table— "Is that candied pineapple you're eating?" "Yes, candied. Under a salt crust." A couple of first-time diners wax rhapsodic as they leave: "We felt as though everyone in the room was a personal friend." Others linger on. As the afternoon shadows lengthen, they gather

Top to bottom:
*Beets from Alain Passard's own
vegetable garden on the banks
of the Loire.
Precision is a byword
in the kitchens.
The chef is especially proud of
his bread, which is baked fresh
every morning.*

Facing page:
*Minimalism combined with
respect for the past—Alain's
grandmother still keeps a vigi-
lant eye on the dining room.*

around a single table, joking with the chef, who's joined them, sipping Calvados, puffing on cigars. It's a great salon, perhaps the greatest salon on Paris's Left Bank. Passard explains a policy of his that helps set the tone: "I refuse to have valet parking, which means I don't have to put up with people who rush in for a business lunch and want to be out again by three o'clock sharp."

Portions are small. Passard claims it only takes a few bites to get a sense of each successive dish. This way, interest remains high right through to the end of the meal. What is this exactly? Not the old appetizer-main-dish-dessert routine, that's for sure. Passard has raised the element of surprise to an esthetic imperative. "It's like a theatrical play. Each act has to develop the action on the basis of the preceding ones." His latest passion is bread. Bread with an airy crumb, golden crust, and a slight taste of yeast. He serves it plain, in slices. There's no need for the folderol often seen in this type of restaurant— nut rolls, raisin buns, and the addition of heaven-knows-what spices. Passard is sure enough of himself to keep things simple. His last words are: "I know what I'm doing, and I just do it."

THE REGION

In addition to the Rue de Varenne staff, L'Arpège has two employees located in…Sarthe. Two gardeners who ensure that Alain Passard's dreams will bear fruit. They don't just shove any old leek, celery, or turnip plant into the ground. Month after month, they select the most flavorful varieties, the ones most suitable to the local soil. This is meticulous work. "I want to create vintage vegetables on a par with vintage wines." Alain Passard even sends members of his Paris staff down to the country every once in a while to pull up the odd onion or carrot themselves. It seems they return from these excursions bursting with fresh enthusiasm and new ideas. According to Passard, inspiration comes directly from the raw product.

This attitude developed gradually, naturally. Passard had always been known for his discriminating eye at the market. His restaurant featured milk-fed veal and lamb chops, along with the best lobsters from Brittany, scallops from Erquy, and chickens, again from Brittany, that are allowed to roam out-of-doors for at least six months before going into the pot. "I'm lucky. I'm a local boy and I have lots of friends in Brittany." However, even an address book full of reliable contacts couldn't protect him from the mad-cow crisis. "No chef worth his salt could ignore the facts. We were like architects who suddenly realize the wood they're using is full of termites." And perhaps, unconsciously, he was looking for an excuse to reinvent himself. Which is exactly what he did. He's now close to being a vegetarian, and a happy one. "I feel as though a whole new life is opening out in front of me. A whole new world to explore."

He's not dogmatic. He still serves free-range poultry, shellfish supplied by his friends in Brittany, and the occasional squab. But vegetables are the stars. Celery root is served in a salt crust opened by the maître d'hôtel with the same reverence shown to sea bass or capon. Sweet onions from the Cévennes are delicately folded into a gratin seasoned with a hint of sage. At L'Arpège, you're likely to hear your dinner partner exclaim rapturously, "It's wild. This is a potato. Just a plain old potato. But it's marvelous!" The meal ends with a preserved-tomato dessert. As Alain Passard explains, "There are no such things as lowly products and noble ones. Just good products and bad."

THE STYLE

It's a look. Attentive, almost aggressive, like a painter deciding on the few strokes he'll make to transform matter and color into a work of art. When we watch Alain Passard at work, we see an artist in action. Concentration. A joyful gleam of the eye when things go right. An agile hand stirring broth. A flick of the fingers setting a pot firmly on the burner, just there and nowhere else, to a fraction of an inch, or else the mussels won't be cooked properly. Nothing

is left to chance. Chefs are manipulators of fire, masters of burner and oven. The possibilities at Passard's are limitless, because everything is under control. Ranged around him, the members of his staff are more than just assistants—they're inventors.

Alain Passard apprenticed in the old school before spearheading the avant-garde. "I worked with all the greatest chefs. I was trained in the entire repertory of French cuisine." Thoroughly versed in the classics, a veteran of banquets, weddings, and baptisms, he knows exactly how far he can go and when. He may work on the margins of current fashion, but he never overdoes it. When he designs a checkerboard using strips of scallop and truffles, the ingredients are raw and thinly sliced, but you don't for a moment imagine you're in Japan. This is definitely the seventh arrondissement of Paris.

Passard's dishes are built on solid foundations, but the details change constantly. In the dining room he's an attentive host, stopping to chat with his guests and returning periodically to the kitchen to make adjustments to the dishes being prepared there. He claims he has to know exactly who's sitting at each table in order to work effectively. When he's found out who you are and what you like, he may bring you something entirely different from what you ordered. Not that the menu is very explicit. It includes terse headings such as "The Egg," "The Périgord Noir Truffle," and "Shellfish from the Bay of Mont-Saint-Michel." The appropriate context for these items will be invented for you by Passard, and Passard alone.

Page 138:
The discreet beauty of
Lalique glass.

Page 139:
The chef improvises. Here,
nothing is standardized; every-
thing is continually reinvented.

France's National Assembly is
right across the street.

Facing page:
The starting gun.

SERVES 8
- 8 eggs
- Fleur de sel
- 1 bunch chives
- 1 cup 45% fat-content
  heavy cream
- 1 tablespoon good sherry
  vinegar
- Mixed spice
- Maple syrup for decoration

PREPARATION TIME
35 minutes

COOKING TIME
10 minutes

In the kitchen.

Hot-and-Cold Eggs with Chives

Using a pair of scissors, cut the tops off the eggs and pour out the whites, leaving the yolks in the shell.

Season the yolks with a pinch of fleur de sel and a teaspoon of chopped chives.

Whip the cream with the sherry vinegar. Add a dash of mixed spice and a pinch of fleur de sel. Chill.

Place the egg shells containing the yolks on a rack in a pan of water heated to a temperature of 140°F to 145°F (60° to 62°C). Keep the temperature steady and coddle the eggs for 8 minutes. Remove the shells from the rack and place them in individual eggcups.

Using a spoon or a pastry bag, fill each eggshell to the rim with the whipped cream mixture. Decorate with a dash of maple syrup.

Green Salad Tartlets

SERVES 4
- 5 oz ready-to-bake puff pastry dough
- 1 head cos lettuce
- 8 oakleaf lettuce leaves
- A few leaves curly chicory lettuce
- A few leaves of lamb's lettuce
- 1 sprig dill
- 4 sprigs chervil
- 5 chives
- 1 tablespoon olive oil
- Juice of ¼ lemon
- Salt, pepper

PREPARATION TIME
20 minutes

COOKING TIME
30 minutes

Preheat the oven to 325°F (160°C).

On a flat surface, roll out the pastry dough to a thickness of about 1/5 inch (½ cm). Cut small rounds from the dough with a cookie cutter and line small tart pans with them. Keep the dough below the rim of the pans. Place another tart pan over the one containing the dough and weight with dried beans to prevent the pastry from bulging.

Bake for 25 minutes, checking the color occasionally.

Wash and trim the lettuce. Remove the cooked pastry shells from the pans and allow to cool. Press the lettuce leaves together into a roll and chop finely. Place the chopped lettuce in a bowl. Wash, wipe, and chop the herbs. Add the herbs to the chopped salad. Season to taste and dress with the olive oil and lemon juice. Fill the pastry shells generously with the salad mixture, piling as high as possible. Serve immediately.

Beechwood-Smoked Potatoes

SERVES 2
- 4 medium potatoes
- ½ lb beechwood chips
- 1 bunch flat parsley
- 1 tablespoon unsalted butter
- Fleur de sel
- 1 sweet Cévennes onion
- 3 tablespoons salted butter
- ⅓ cup water

PREPARATION TIME
35 minutes

COOKING TIME
1 hour 30 minutes

Cover the potatoes with cold salted water, bring to the boil, lower heat, and simmer for 45 minutes. When the potatoes are cooked, place them in a beechwood smoker for 30 minutes.

Stem the parsley and cook in boiling salted water for 3 minutes. Mix the parsley in the blender with 2 tablespoons salted butter and ⅓ cup of the water it was cooked in. Blend for 5 minutes, season to taste with fleur de sel, strain.

Peel and chop the onion. Melt the remaining 2 tablespoons of salted butter in a saucepan, add the onion and ⅓ cup water. Simmer for 10 minutes. Mix in blender, season to taste and strain.

To assemble the dish, make a circle with the parsley mixture on each plate. Peel the potatoes and cut in half lengthwise. Place two of the halved potatoes in the middle of each parsley circle.

Dribble a little of the onion sauce around the potatoes and parsley. Garnish the potatoes with a dab of unsalted butter and season with fleur de sel. Serve hot.

Cabbage Stuffed with Spring Vegetables

Wash and peel the vegetables. Bring a pot of water to the boil, add 1 tablespoon salted butter and the vegetables, dropping them in the water one-by-one: first the turnip, then the carrots, celery, and potato.

Do not peel the onion and shallots, but cut them in two lengthwise. Place in a frying pan with 2 tablespoons of the butter and sauté over low heat for 1 hour 30 minutes, stirring occasionally.

Place the cabbage leaves in another frying pan, adding 2 tablespoons of the butter and 2 tablespoons of water. Cook, covered, for 6 minutes. The cabbage should remain crisp.

Stem the bunch of flat parsley and cook in boiling salted water for 3 minutes. Mix in blender with 3 tablespoons of the butter and ⅓ cup of the cooking water. Season to taste with the fleur de sel and strain.

For the onion sauce, peel and chop one of the sautéed onion halves. In a pot, melt the remaining 2 tablespoons of butter with ⅓ cup water. Add the chopped onion and simmer for 10 minutes. Mix in blender, season to taste, and press through a strainer.

Peel the other sautéed onion half and the shallots, shred in a food processor with all the other vegetables except the cabbage.

Arrange mounds of the shredded vegetables on each of four warmed plates. Sprinkle with fleur de sel, a dash of lemon juice, and the chopped parsley.

Season the cabbage leaves lightly with pepper and place one leaf on either side of the vegetable mounds.

Pour a thin stream of the parsley and onion sauces around each plate.

SERVES 4
- 1 "Boule d'Or" turnip
- 1 yellow carrot
- 1 orange carrot
- ¼ of a celery root
- 1 potato
- 4 oz salted butter
- 1 Cévennes sweet onion
- 4 gray shallots
- 8 cabbage leaves
- 1 bunch flat parsley, plus one tablespoon chopped flat parsley for garnish
- ⅓ cup water
- A few drops lemon juice
- Freshly ground pepper, fleur de sel

PREPARATION TIME
1 hour

COOKING TIME
2 hours

At the end of their shift, servers take a moment to glimpse Paris life.

Fabien : Est ce que les commandes de lait et de beurre on été faite. Il faut 5 kg beurre 1/2 sel

Twelve-Spice Tomato Conserve

SERVES 4
- 4 tomatoes
- ½ lb apples
- ½ lb pears
- 5 tablespoons pineapple
- 1 teaspoon fresh ginger
- 1 tablespoon walnuts
- 1 tablespoon almonds
- 1 tablespoon pistachios
- ½ teaspoon orange peel
- 1 teaspoon lemon peel
- 1 tablespoon brown sugar
- 4 cloves
- ½ teaspoon cinnamon
- 15 Corinth raisins
- ¼ teaspoon mint
- 2 vanilla pods
- ½ teaspoon grated star anise
- 1 tablespoon granulated sugar
- Juice of 1 orange
- 4 scoops vanilla ice cream

PREPARATION TIME
40 minutes

COOKING TIME
2 hours

Preheat oven to 400°F (200°C).

Shred the apples, pears, pineapple, ginger, walnuts, almonds, and pistachios. Cut the orange and lemon peel into julienne strips.

Caramelize the brown sugar in a frying pan, add the apples, pears, and pineapple. Sauté over high heat until almost cooked. Add the orange and lemon peel, ginger, cloves, cinnamon, raisins, chopped mint, walnuts, almonds, pistachios, and one of the vanilla beans (split and scraped) and the star anise.

Cut the tops off the tomatoes, remove the seeds and membrane. Fill the hollow tomatoes with the fruit stuffing.

Caramelize the granulated sugar in a small frying pan, add the orange juice and the remaining vanilla pod (split and scraped).

Place the orange juice and tomatoes in a frying pan, simmer over low heat for 2 hours. Stir frequently to prevent the mixture from sticking or burning.

Serve with the pan juices and a scoop of vanilla ice cream.

Pineapple in Salt Crust

SERVES 1
- 1 Victoria pineapple weighing about ½ lb
- 4 lbs coarse Guérande salt
- 4 oranges
- 3 tablespoons sugar
- ½ Tahiti vanilla bean

PREPARATION TIME
40 minutes

COOKING TIME
1 hour 15 minutes

Preheat oven to 300°F (150°C).

On a baking sheet, build up a mound of coarse salt. Scoop a hollow out of the mound, leaving the base and sides about 1½-inches (4 cm) thick. Bury the pineapple in the salt, covering it completely except for the leaves. Bake for 1 hour 15 minutes.

When done, allow to rest at room temperature for 1 hour.

Squeeze the oranges. In a saucepan, combine the orange juice with the sugar and the ½ vanilla bean (split and scraped). Stir and reduce by one-half.

To serve, bring the pineapple to the table in its salt crust.

Carefully cut away the crust, then peel the pineapple.

Cut the pineapple flesh crossways into thin slices and arrange the slices in circles on individual plates.

Cover with the orange-juice reduction.

Serve hot.

Page 148:
One of the day's many orders to staff.

Page 149:
A pirouette executed by Alain Passard:
tomato preserve as a dessert.

GÉRALD PASSÉDAT

LE PETIT NICE

MARSEILLES

THE MAN

This is a spot that could easily upstage the man; it is one of the most beautiful in Marseilles. The view from the terrace of sea, port, Corniche, Cap Croisette, and distant islands. After sundown, it is a view garlanded with lights and murmuring with the sounds of the city. A palm and a few plane trees around the swimming pool set the tone, creating a rural, turn-of-the-century atmosphere. This is downtown Marseilles, but it could be the Riviera during the era of British and Russian princesses. Gérald Passédat is a local boy, and proud of it. At soccer games he sits with the Ultras, the Olympique de Marseilles' most rabid supporters. He stays out till dawn during the Dock Fiesta, a typically boisterous Marseilles event. "I was one of the first people to believe in the future of this city. Twenty years ago no one was talking about Guédiguian or Izzo, and everyone I knew advised me to make a life for myself somewhere else. But I stuck it out. I was inspired by a trip to New York, when some friends took me to SoHo and TriBeca. That's when I realized that we had exactly the same thing here, in miniature."

Actually, this man, who was conventionally brought up in a respectable middle-class family, is anything but sophisticated. He hates cocktail parties. When he takes a break from his kitchen, he'd rather go out on the town with his buddies. This hasn't done anything to hone his image. "I just couldn't be bothered with Marseilles high society and the media. It's true that I'm often not as diplomatic as I should be." But what we have here is something worth knowing about: a restaurant in Marseilles—a city of gastronomes—that has been in the same family since 1907 and is run by a forty-year-old chef who maintains the old traditions and is also a mine of inventiveness.

He learned his first lessons as a child, when he'd hover around the pots that his two grandmothers—one Corsican, the other Catalonian—had simmering on the stove.

He went on to perfect his art with the best Parisian chefs. His own character did the rest. "In the late 1970s, deciding to be a chef wasn't quite the thing. It was better to be a doctor, a lawyer—or even a gangster." When Gérald returned home to take over Le Petit Nice, he was able to keep the two Michelin stars won by his father. And to hope for more. He's a truly creative spirit, inventive and curious. He is one of those chefs who, in his own words, put all of their "rage" into their cuisine.

THE REGION

Passédat's native soil is the sea. He's had it in front of his eyes since earliest childhood. He grew up beside the sea, in the dining room of a restaurant located in midtown but overlooking a strip of cove with waves crashing on the rocks. Gérald Passédat is a seaside chef. As a dyed-in-the-wool Marseillais, he identifies more with the sky and sea than with the inland Provençal countryside. He willingly admits that the vegetable appetizers featured on his menu are there simply to "satisfy our organic cravings." He goes on to explain, "I was tired of listening to foreigners ask for salads." And the three meat dishes he offers, although perfect, are not his highest priority either. "One of these days I'll just start cooking nothing but fish."

Preceding double page:
Le Petit Nice-Passédat, a classic
on the Marseilles Corniche.

A discussion in the kitchen.

Facing page:
No doubt about it: this fish was
caught last night,
with a rod and line.

Gérald Passédat doesn't go to the central fish market: the fishermen come to him. They drive or sail by every day before setting up their stands in the Vieux Port. There are only a few who've won Gérard's approbation, and the old craft is disappearing. But there are still enough stalwarts to set up a brilliant display on the Petit Nice terrace: fresh sea bass, denti, red rock mullet, sea anemones, squillfish (sea grasshoppers), crayfish, sea urchins, violet sea snails. Rare products. Precious ones.

Just between ourselves, we agree that these fish and crustaceans caught fresh from the Mediterranean Sea are vastly superior to their cousins from the Atlantic Ocean. And even more so when prepared by Gérald, without butter or cream, just olive oil. It is always the same oil, pressed at a small Provençal mill. "Every year I sample other oils in blind tastings, but I always come back to this one." No sauces, just natural pan juices, reductions, infusions. And he also goes easy on the herbs—that Provençal cliché. Passédat proves the Marseilles authenticity of his cuisine through subtle allusion. Artichokes as the garnish for a denti, a few strips of truffle decorating a fillet of sea bass. Perfect balance is the keynote, from the geometric plates to the meticulous techniques enhancing the interplay of flavors.

THE STYLE

First, sea urchins in every way, shape, and form; sea urchins like you've never seen before. Pure coral that melts in the mouth, to be eaten with a spoon or served on crusty pastry. Coral to drink, sip, or combine with the other things on the plate—scallops or a mousse of violet sea snails. And then, sea-anemone fritters, transporting us for an instant to Szechuan. Or fillets of red rock mullet with an unusual dusting of pistachios. We're off! This is Marseilles as the gateway to the East, the Mediterranean, a whole new world.

Then, in the middle of the meal, Passédat presents his own special refresher course. It's served automatically, without being ordered, and comes in an oversize stemmed glass. A drink both hot and cold, potato consommé garnished with a dollop of light and foamy fish soup, well-seasoned with saffron. This delight for the eye should be swallowed all at once, thus releasing the full power of its subtle evocations: kitchens remembered from childhood, fishing boats returning to port, fish soup and wine savored in a cabin by the sea. Memories of an entire city, an entire generation. All too soon it's gone, but its melody lingers on. Now here comes the denti, cooked in suckling-pig juices.

That gives you some idea of Gérald Passédat's cuisine, which is an evocative quest for new alchemies. Passédat isn't known for bouillabaisse, but his guests keep on asking him for it. Which annoys him. So he invents something new. He once pressed bouillabaisse into a terrine—a sort of compressed cliché in the city of auto-compression sculptor César. Today Passédat deconstructs his bouillabaisse, dividing it among a dozen little molds. It's still bouillabaisse, all right, but cubist. And all his own.

Facing page:
Working at full speed.

Top to bottom:
A dish of culinary spices.
Saffron pistils, a costly ingredient.
Turnovers.

SERVES 4
- 8 sea anemones
- 2 lb clams
- 2 lb sea scallops
- 4 periwinkles
- Wine vinegar
- Peanut oil
- Parsley
- ¾ cup balsamic vinegar, ideally aged
- Salt
- Juice of 1 lemon

For the fritter batter
- 2 cups flour
- 5 egg yolks
- 1½ cups beer
- Salt, pepper

PREPARATION TIME
45 minutes

COOKING TIME
3-5 minutes

Entrance to the Old Port.

An Ocean Medley of Sea-Anemone Fritters and Tender "Szechuan" Shellfish

Rinse all the shellfish, except for the periwinkles, and place in large pot over medium heat, cover, and cook until the shells open. Remove from heat. Strain the cooking liquid and set aside in the refrigerator.

To prepare the fritter batter, place the flour in a bowl. Beat in the egg yolks and enough beer to make a smooth dough (consistency of pancake batter). Add salt and pepper to taste.

Remove the cooked shellfish meat from the shells and heat in the cooking liquid and a little lemon juice.

Dip the sea anemones in the wine vinegar, drain. Chop, and then coat with the fritter batter. Deep-fry for 5 minutes in peanut oil heated to 350°F (180°C).

Open the periwinkles, cut in half, and remove the meat using the thumb.

Arrange the clams and periwinkles on the plate. Sprinkle with chopped parsley.

Heat the shellfish broth with the balsamic vinegar, pour over the shellfish.

Garnish with the fritters, season with salt and lemon juice.

SERVES 4
- 1 gilt-head bream weighing 3 lb
- Olive oil
- Coarse Camargue salt
- White pepper
- 1 cup fish stock

For the pâté garnish
- 3 oz angler-fish liver
- 3 oz flaked fish
- 1 chopped shallot
- 2 oz spinach sprouts
- 1 tablespoon Noilly Prat Vermouth
- Pinch of 4-spices blend
- 1 tablespoon veal pan juices
- Salt, pepper

For the savory sauce
- 1 cup honey
- 1 cup sherry vinegar
- 3 tablespoons fresh ginger, roughly chopped
- 2 cups veal stock
- Salt, pepper
- 1 eggplant
- Olive oil

PREPARATION TIME
45 minutes

COOKING TIME
35 minutes

The olive oil comes from Les Baux-de-Provence.

Medallions of Gilt-Head Bream Garnished with Eggplant Preserve and Pâté

- *Preparing the gilt-head bream*: Pare, scale, clean, and rinse the fish. Remove the central bone through the stomach, leaving the back intact. Tie the fish like a roast, slice into 4 parts weighing about ½ pound each. Rub with olive oil, season, and set aside.

- *Preparing the pâté garnish*: Preheat oven to 425°F (220 °C). Chop the pâté-garnish ingredients and mix with the fingertips until smooth and thoroughly blended. Press flat, cut into rectangles and place on ovenproof paper. Drizzle with olive oil and bake until cooked.

- *Preparing the savory sauce*: Caramelize the honey in a frying pan. Add ½ cup sherry vinegar and the coarsely chopped ginger, boil until reduced by about one-half and deglaze the pan again, this time with the veal stock.

  Simmer until the mixture becomes slightly syrupy. Season to taste.

  Cut the eggplant into round slices, sauté in olive oil, deglaze with ½ cup sherry vinegar, and add to the savory sauce (above).

Preheat oven to 160°F (70°C).

  Grill the slices of fish just long enough to mark them. Finish by oven-steaming in a little fish stock for 15-28 minutes.

  Allow the fish to rest for a few minutes before serving.

SERVES 4
- 12 rock mullet
- ¼ cup pistachio oil
- 2 cups fish stock
- 1 star anise
- 8 oysters
- Coriander leaves
- ½ cup crushed pistachios
- Salt, pepper

PREPARATION TIME
50 minutes

COOKING TIME
5 minutes

Oriental Mullet and Oyster Consommé with Shellfish and a Pistachio Topping

Preheat oven to 425° (220°C).

Pare, scale, and clean the mullet. Remove the livers and the fillets (six per person). Using tweezers, bone the fillets.

Heat the bones in the pistachio oil, and add the fish stock. Strain, add the star anise and set aside.

Mix the livers in a blender with a little of the seasoned stock and set aside.

Open the oysters and poach them in their juice.

Bake half of the mullet fillets, drizzled with olive oil, in the hot oven. Poach the rest of the fillets in the stock.

Place the poached fillets and the oysters in a soup plate, cover with the broth, and add a few coriander petals.

Dredge the baked mullet fillets in the crushed pistachios, and dot with a little of the liver purée and a dash of pistachio oil.

Gérald grew up along these coves that reach into the center of town.

SERVES 4

For the caramelized basil
• 1 cup fondant icing
• ½ cup glucose
• 1 tablespoon chopped basil

For the sparkling orange powder
• 1 orange
• 1 tablespoon sherbet powder

For the fruit purée
• Mango, pear, kiwi
  (depending on the season)

For the milk chiffon
• 2 cups milk
• 4½ sheets of gelatin
• Rind of 1 lime

1 sponge cake

PREPARATION TIME
1 hour

COOKING TIME
20 minutes

A consciously elegant establishment.

Barley Sugar with Fruit Purée

• *Preparing the caramelized-basil rolls:* Preheat oven to 425°F (220°C). Heat the fondant icing and glucose to a temperature of 320°F (158°C), add the chopped basil, blend thoroughly and then spread on ovenproof paper to cool. Place the paper holding the caramelized basil in the oven and heat until it melts. Remove from oven, cover with a second sheet of ovenproof paper, and press gently to spread evenly.

Cut the caramel into rectangles measuring about 2 ½ × 1 inch (6 × 3 cm) and roll them around a cylindrical mold of about ½ inch (15mm) in diameter to form tubes. Set the remaining scraps of caramelized basil aside for later.

• *Preparing the sparkling orange powder:* Cut the rind of 1 orange into julienne strips, blanch 3 times in boiling water, roll in melted sugar, and allow to dry in a cool spot.

When the pieces of candied orange rind are dry, mix in blender with the sherbet powder.

• *Preparing the fruit purée*: Peel the raw fruit and purée each one, separately, in the blender.

• *Preparing the milk chiffon*: Soften the sheets of gelatin in a little cold water. Heat half of the milk and add the gelatin, stirring until dissolved. Add the rind of 1 lime, stir, allow to set partially. Whip in the remaining cold milk. Shape into a cylinder.

• *Preparing the caramelized-basil base*: Pulverize the remaining scraps of caramelized-basil in the blender.

Plug one end of the caramelized-basil tubes with a small disk of sponge-cake. Fill the tube with successive layers of the different fruit purées, then plug the other end with a second sponge-cake disk. Arrange a square of the caramelized-basil powder on a plate and top with a filled tube.

Cut the milk chiffon into 2-inch (5 cm) cylinders. Roll the cylinders in the sparkling orange powder and place on the edge of the plate.

ANNE-SOPHIE PIC

CHEZ PIC

VALENCE

THE WOMAN

There are two chapters to this story. The first—at her own family's famed institution—lasted all of nine months, after which Anne-Sophie decided it was too much for her. She'd never been to catering school, never apprenticed, never worked at a great restaurant. All she had was a diploma from a Parisian business school. Understandably, when the prodigal child returned and tried to play chef, the old-timers didn't take her seriously. Her elder brother was already in charge; her father died suddenly; the fledgling artist still had a lot to learn. It was too soon. She knew it, retired from the scene and, with her husband, created the comfortable hotel that had always been lacking at the Pic family's place. The story's second chapter began in 1999, when she tried again. Meanwhile, the restaurant had lost one of its three Michelin stars. Anne-Sophie returned to the fray. This time she listened to her elders, while also imposing her own vision. Win or lose. She won.

In the Pic household, new departures are the rule. The family saga began with a great-grandmother who ran the Auberge du Pin in a little Ardèche village while her husband tilled the fields. It was a country café serving game pâté and other simple fare. Her son—Anne-Sophie's grandfather—followed much the same path as Anne-Sophie. He didn't take over from his parents right away. He wanted to see what was going on in the world, so he went to Paris to learn the trade. It was an experience that transformed his idea of cuisine. As a result, he won three Michelin stars in 1934, just one year after the guide was first published. That's when he moved to Valence, in the Drôme. The street on which the restaurant stands—the Avenue Victor Hugo, bordered by open fields—is also the N7, national highway to the Riviera. In the era before expressways and high-speed trains, Pic, like Troisgros in Roanne, became a popular stop for motorists traveling south. Curnonsky recognized its quality with a compliment that has since become legendary: "There are three creative spirits in modern cuisine: Dumaine, Pic, and Point."

And yet Anne-Sophie's father only narrowly missed spending his whole life as an auto mechanic. All things come to an end, even the most ambitious dreams, and the grandfather eventually lost two of his stars. It was Anne-Sophie's mother who saved the day. She persuaded her husband to give up car repair and stick with the restaurant, even if he had to begin all over again. He did have talent, and he rose to the challenge. His truffle turnovers and sea bass with caviar became famous throughout France. Anne-Sophie still prepares them, according to the old recipe, as a tribute. And they still underlie her philosophy: "My father was an inventive chef for his time." This is a subtle way of rationalizing her own approach—never mind the customers who complain that things aren't the same as before. Anne-Sophie has stamped the menu with her own mark.

This slip of a woman is stubborn. Although lavish in her praise of Alain Passard and Michel Bras, she bases her own inspiration on her own instincts. "I chose this field because I want to be creative." Now that she's sure of her professional skills, she describes herself as serene. "At first, I had to test my authority. My role model was my father, and I used to scream and yell the way he did. Today, I'm self-confident enough to ask my assistants for advice. I use tact. I try to stay feminine." With the disappearance of the famed "Mères" of Lyon and the rise of today's great male chefs, Anne-Sophie Pic is one of the few French women working in the field today.

THE REGION

Anne-Sophie's father didn't actually teach her how to cook, but he honed her tastes. "As a tiny girl, I always had the best bread, butter, and chocolate in my schoolbag for my recess snack. Much to my despair, I was never allowed to eat commercial cookies. We often ate out in restaurants as a family, and my father always analyzed every detail of the meal. When I was studying in Paris, he'd send me back from trips home with little delicacies in Tupperware containers." The heir to generations of

*Salsify and crisp salads—
vegetables are a treasure
of the Rhône valley.*

professional gourmets, Anne-Sophie's tastes developed through high gastronomy rather than plain country cooking. This explains why, in the heart of the Drôme, she's totally at ease with seafood. "There was always seafood at my father's, and that's why fish is my primary culinary specialty today."

Meanwhile, she's learned to draw on the surrounding countryside. To turn not only toward the coast but also inland, toward Lyon, a city no chef can ignore. The region is a rich one, midway between the land of olive oil and the land of cream, the sere aromatic slopes of the south and the dark forests of the Vercors, Beaujolais, and Côte du Rhône. Anne-Sophie used to spend her vacations in Ardèche and the Alpes-de-Haute-Provence. She now believes that the cuisine of Provence suits modern lifestyles better than that of Lyon. That's her bias. Her bistro, L'Auberge du Pin, is frankly Provençal. The dining rooms of her gastronomic restaurant are more conventional, more refined, but just as appealing.

Anne-Sophie Pic's menu features Rémuzat lamb with a hint of aromatic southern herbs, chestnuts, and hare from the Ardèche, Puy lentils and Mediterranean sea urchins, and Picodon and Sassenage blue cheese from the nearby Vercors. She offers truffles in season, since the black "Périgord" truffle is a regional specialty. "My father served truffles cooked. My generation serves them raw, seasoned with a dash of olive oil and a pinch of fleur de sel." To these local products she adds Salers beef, duck from l'Huppe and even potatoes from Monsieur Clos, a lord of the superb ratte variety, who works out of Brie. Anne-Sophie's region is the whole of France.

The Vercors mountains on the outskirts of Valence.

Page 172:
The lettuce comes straight from Jean-Luc Reillon, a neighboring produce farmer.

Page 173:
The dining room, viewed from the wings like a stage set.

THE STYLE

Anne-Sophie believes progress is based on the development of personal taste. Season after season, her own menu reflects her travels, discoveries, and personal favorites. Recently she's been building thematic compositions based on a single flavor; evocations of warm summer days, of sunny vacations. For example, she recently composed a shellfish plate around the sharp tang of sea spray. This is just one example of how this artist is gradually moving away from the immutable traditions of conventional French cuisine—her roots—in order to embark on more personal journeys.

Anne-Sophie Pic's cuisine is full of flavor, but it's also light. She uses emulsions, reductions, and aspics, of course, but also techniques borrowed from all the cuisines of the world. Scallops are grilled Barcelona-style, known as a la plancha. Sea bass is steamed with Wakamé as in Kyoto, and beef ravioli are served in a borsch-type consommé. Most dishes are enhanced with small, lavish details. The terms palet (puck), bonbon (piece of candy), calisson (almond candy), tuile (thin sweet cookie), and mousseline appear frequently on her menu. She calls this the feminine side of her cuisine.

But Anne-Sophie Pic respects her roots. Although she continuously welcomes new guests to her table, not all of them are willing to embark on this personal journey of discovery. That's fine with her. She sees it as a necessary rein on her creativity. "People should be surprised, but not too surprised. That is, if you want them to make a return visit. At Pic, I take as much care with the standard menu, featuring traditional dishes, as with the tasting menus, for which I allow myself much more freedom."

Below:
Turnips with Spiced Caramel (recipe page 176).

Below right:
Honing a new recipe—to within a fraction of an inch.

Facing page:
Valence lies between the Lyon region and Provence, but Anne-Sophie Pic favors the South.

Truffle in Pastry "André Pic"

SERVES 6
- ½ lb ready-to-bake puff pastry
- 6 large truffles (about 1 oz each)
- 6 small, very thin slices of bacon (maximum ⅛-inch thick)
- ⅔ tablespoon reduced pan juices from a roast
- 1 egg yolk
- Salt, freshly ground pepper

PREPARATION TIME
40 minutes

COOKING TIME
25 minutes

Preheat oven to 350°F (180°C).

Roll out the pastry to a thickness of ⅛ inch (6 mm).

Using a round serrated cookie cutter, cut two identical disks from the pastry, each measuring about 5 inches (12 cm) in diameter.

Peel the truffles and set the pieces of peel aside. Dip the peeled truffles in the pan juices, wrap each one with a slice of bacon, and place them all on one of the pastry disks. Cover with the second pastry disk. Moisten the edges of the pastry with a little water and press to seal. Brush with egg yolk.

Brown the turnover for 5 minutes, increase the oven heat to 425°F (220°C), and continue baking for 10 to 15 minutes more until done.

Serve the pastry accompanied by a green salad garnished with the pieces of truffle peel.

Turnips with Spiced Caramel

SERVES 4
- 1 long white turnip
- 4 oz lump sugar
- ½ teaspoon "4-spice" mixture
- ¼ cup water
- Fleur de sel, freshly ground pepper

PREPARATION TIME
30 minutes

COOKING TIME
40 minutes

Wash and pare the turnip.

Cut into slices ⅓-inch (1 cm) thick and trim with a cookie cutter.

Parboil the disks of turnip in boiling salted water, refresh, and drain on absorbent paper.

Lightly caramelize the sugar with the 4-spice mixture and about ¼ cup water in a frying pan.

Add the turnips and stir over a low heat until caramelized.

When the turnips are cogolden, remove from heat and season with a little fleur de sel and freshly ground pepper.

SERVES 8
- 4 lb cuttlefish (squid is also suitable for this dish, but is less flavorful)
- 5 oz red onions
- 5 oz leeks
- 5 oz carrots
- 5 oz celery
- 2 cloves garlic, chopped
- Sprig of fresh thyme
- ¼ bunch chervil
- ¼ bunch parsley
- ¼ bunch coriander
- Pinch of ground saffron

- 1 oz shallots, peeled and chopped
- Olive oil
- 2 tablespoons white balsamic vinegar
- ¼ bunch chives

PREPARATION TIME
45 minutes

COOKING TIME
25 minutes

Table settings.

Marinated Cuttlefish with Crisp Vegetables

Clean and rinse the cuttlefish, cut into strips, drain.

Peel the onions and cut into petals. Pare and trim the other vegetables, cut into julienne strips.

Briefly sauté all the vegetables in olive oil with one chopped garlic clove and the thyme.

The vegetables should remain crisp. Drain the sautéed vegetables, cool slightly. Wash and crush the chervil, parsley, coriander and saffron. Cover the vegetables with olive oil, then add the crushed herbs.

Sauté the cuttlefish in olive oil heated to smoking point in a nonstick frying pan. Add the second chopped garlic clove and shallots. Drain and cover with vinaigrette dressing made with olive oil, white balsamic vinegar, and chopped chives.

Place a mound of the crisp vegetables on each plate. Top with the cuttlefish and serve.

Rock Sea Urchins in the Shell with Granny-Smith Apple Cream

Soften the gelatin in cold water.

Use a pair of scissors to open the sea urchins. Scoop out the flesh with a demi-tasse spoon. Set aside 5 pieces of sea-urchin flesh for the garnish. Strain the juice and cool in the refrigerator. Carefully rinse the shells under a stream of warm water.

In a bowl, mix the egg, egg yolks, milk, remaining pieces of sea-urchin flesh, and the liquid from the shells. Blend in a food processor and season.

Place this mixture in the sea-urchin shells, filling three-quarters of the way up. Cook the filled shells for about 15 minutes in a steam oven heated to 175°F (80°C).

Cover with plastic film and chill.

Heat 1⅓ cups of the apple juice and the lemon juice in a saucepan with the softened gelatin and the agar-agar. Whisk to blend. Add the rest of the apple juice and chill.

Place mounds of coarse salt on small serving plates. Press the filled sea urchins firmly into the salt. Garnish each shell with the whipped apple cream, decorate with a stick of green apple and a sliver of sea-urchin flesh. Serve chilled.

SERVES 5
- 10 sea urchins
- 1 egg & 3 yolks
- ½ cup milk
- Liquid from the sea-urchin shells
- Salt, pepper
- Green apple for garnish

For the granny-smith apple cream
- 2 cups green-apple juice
- 1 teaspoon gelatin
- ¼ oz agar-agar (seaweed thickener available from health-food stores)
- Juice of ½ lemon
- Coarse salt

PREPARATION TIME
45 minutes

COOKING TIME
10 minutes

The final touch before a dish is sent out to the dining room.

SERVES 4
- 2 mangoes
- 2 large pieces phyllo dough
- 2 teaspoons confectioners' sugar
- ½ pint vanilla ice cream or ½ pint mango sorbet

For the poaching syrup
- 3 tablespoons sugar
- ⅓ cup water
- ½ vanilla pod

For the lemon cream
- 3 tablespoons pastry cream (see recipe page 214)
- 1 tablespoon peeled lemon sections, crushed
- 1 sheet gelatin
- 3 tablespoons heavy cream

For the sugar crisps
- 3 tablespoons water
- ½ cup sugar
- 3 tablespoons glucose
- ½ vanilla pod

PREPARATION TIME
1 hour 30 minutes

COOKING TIME
40 minutes

To remove the last little wrinkle, tablecloths are re-ironed after being spread on the table.

Candied Vanilla Mango, Sugar Crisps with Lemon Cream and Vanilla Ice Cream or Mango Sorbet

• *Preparing the sugar crisps*: Preheat oven to 400°F (200°C). Combine all the ingredients for the crisps in a saucepan and cook to a temperature of 300°F (150°C). Remove from heat and pour the cooked sugar onto a sheet of paper. Cool.

Pulverize the cooled sugar in a food processor. Spread this powder on ovenproof paper and melt in oven. Remove from oven and spread as evenly as possible on a fresh piece of paper. Cut the sugar into four squares while still hot and roll around a cylindrical mold. Allow to harden.

Make a poaching syrup with the water, sugar, and ½ vanilla pod (split and scraped).

Peel the mangoes and cut into thin slices. Poach in the boiling syrup for 5 to 8 minutes. Drain. Using a cookie cutter, cut small disks from the mango slices. Cut the remaining bits of mango into small cubes.

Thin the pastry cream with the lemon flesh. Soften the gelatin in cold water. Whip the cream. Drain the gelatin, melt in a little cream and blend with the lemon pastry-cream mixture. Fold in the whipped cream.

To serve fill the sugar crisps with a layer of lemon cream, a layer of mango, another layer of cream. End with some of the chopped mango.

Cut the phyllo dough into 8 squares, place on baking sheet, and bake for 5 minutes. Trim the cooked pastry to the same size as the mango disks. Sprinkle the disks with sugar and caramelize in the oven. Place one mango disk between two rounds of phyllo pastry, making four "sandwiches" in all. Place one filled sugar tube on each plate, add one of the mango "sandwiches," moisten with a tablespoon of the poaching syrup, and garnish with a spoonful of vanilla ice cream or mango sorbet.

PIERROT

LE BISTROT DE PIERROT

LILLE

THE MAN

Pierrot is a man of the North—a real one. A man who likes to wander over the dunes after the tourists have packed their bags, whose natural element is daylong mist and drizzle, who at nightfall drops into little cafés where he can raise a glass among friends.

Whether striding along the beach or leaning against a bar, Pierrot stands out, both in the way he talks (loudly and clearly) and his size—he is close to six-feet-six and weighs an extra two pounds every year, according to his own reckoning. He also attracts attention because of his fame: Pierrot is a local celebrity and signs autographs by the barrelful.

His media career began when he met Pierre Bonte, also a native of Lille and a veteran of the airwaves. In conjunction with this broadcasting professional, Pierrot launched a daily thirteen-minute telecast on the France 3 Nord television channel. It is still going strong today, but without Pierre Bonte. The rest is history: there followed publishing contracts for cookbooks, trade-show appearances, press coverage, and a line of preserves (with Pierrot's photo on the label), which are sold in supermarkets throughout the region. Just like the chef Joel Robuchon, but in his own domain. Pierrot gets frequent hits on his Web site from customer-pals who want to know, for example, when the next Potato Festival will be held. "I get involved. I love showing off. But my first love is my bistro in Lille."

His bistro is a long, narrow, pocket-handkerchief of a place tucked into the center of Lille. It is full to bursting noon and night, which means it serves about 200 meals per day. It is an institution, a stage where Pierrot performs as flamboyantly as he does on TV, toasting a table-full of friends and slapping local celebrities on the back. Pierrot opened his bistro fifteen years ago, and gave it his first name—nobody ever calls him Monsieur Coucke. Since then he's opened a lot of other businesses, at Le Touquet and elsewhere. But they didn't last. The bistro lasted.

Pierrot learned how to cook the dishes he serves there from "La Mère Simone," his mother, who gets full credit on his menu. She used to run an inn near the Belgian border, in French Flanders, and she's the person who gave Pierrot his taste for calves' headcheese with gribiche sauce, tripe simmered eight hours on the range, roast lamb studded with garlic, and Sunday stewed chicken with rice. "I was never very good in school. But at the age of fourteen, when I trained for my CAP chef's diploma, I was at the top of my class."

To this family training in the flavors and aromas of good food, Pierrot adds his personal warmth, theatrical verve, and childhood memories of the times when he used to spy on the horse-traders cutting deals over a meal at the inn. When all is said and done, he'd rather wear a plain apron in his own dining room than a chef's white coat and hat.

THE REGION

On his TV show, Pierrot often enlivens his recipes with a few words of patois. Rabbit is fully cooked when it's ready to *décafote* (separate from the bone), caramel when it will *guille* (crack between the fingers), and everything should make you *berlafer* (drool). It is just one more way of reminding us that his roots are in the North, a North of meadows and sea, beer and potatoes, France and Belgium.

As a stuffing for tomatoes, Pierrot likes to use the kind of shrimp people snack on during the summer at the beaches of Ostende and La Panne. As he tells it, the sole he serves is *belle*, i.e. fresh and meaty, not sickly, like the poor things you get in Parisian brasseries. It thus has its place on the slate-wall menu alongside hefty items such as andouillettes (chitterling sausage) and pigs' feet and hocks. The regular menu is full of the chef's favorites: heart and liver, veal kidneys, giblets, pork tripe. In Lille, he pioneered the marrow bone sprinkled with coarse salt, back in the days when Guérande salt was not widely used.

Pierrot is also king of the field-grown endive, that tiny lettuce with the distinctive flavor that is grown in chicory country. He was serving pumpkin long before

Preceding double page:
The coastline between
Le Touquet and Bray-Dunes,
from which Pierrot draws his
inspiration.

Left to right:
Tiny Cos lettuces—pearls
from northern soil.
Cheese pie and onion quiche—
typical bistro fare.
Small breweries are making a
strong comeback.

Facing page:
Bintje potatoes from the North,
ideal for French fries.

anyone in Europe had ever heard of Halloween. He also makes fresh French fries from the bintje variety of potato, grown in the loamy soil of the North, reserving the ratte variety from Le Touquet for more refined dishes. "There's been too much hype about local products. I've always used them, but now it's become so trendy it almost makes me feel uncomfortable. People write me asking what kind of potato they should serve with herring. What next!"

Pierrot likes to do things right without going overboard. In beer country, where microbreweries are springing up like mushrooms, he serves only Trois Monts from his beloved Flanders hills, Grain d'Orge, a locally brewed beer that improves with age, and Chti. "That's plenty. Otherwise I'd have to stock more than thirty different beers. I'd never see the end of it."

THE STYLE

A subtle tribute on the menu: next to "Tarte des Demoiselles de Hazebrouk" (two ladies who really do exist, proven by the fact that one of them visited Pierrot to sample her own specialty), Crêpes Suzette are listed with the comment "almost the same as at L'Huîtrière," the large and venerable Lille institution. "Except that it takes Didier, the chef, half an hour to make them." At Pierrot's, things are done swiftly and well. Even when he's performing in the dining room, Pierrot still keeps a keen eye on everything that leaves his kitchen.

Here there are no hard-to-make sauce bases, no complicated preparations. Pierrot does things his own way. A dash of white wine here, a spoonful of brown sugar there. He spent a lot of time observing typical Lyon taverns so he could combine their atmosphere with that of the Flemish neighborhood bar. At Le Bistrot de Pierrot, the menu lists headcheese vinaigrette along with salmon waterzoï, a Flemish version of Marseilles' bouillabaisse. But his two outstanding specialties are truly local: carbonnade—the Flemish boeuf bourguignon, and *potjevleesch*—a cold aspic of pork, chicken, rabbit, and veal. "A dish," Pierrot explains, "that the Dunkerque fishermen used to take with them when they went to sea; a dish that keeps well and is easy to make." Through contacts with local food processors, he has his *potjevleesch* bottled under his own label, and markets it in all of the region's supermarkets. Some day, he promises, he'll reveal the delights of *potjevleesch* to all of France. "Even down on the Riviera, once people taste it, they'll love it. It's refreshing, light. Perfect for hot summer weather. What a great way to introduce the wealth of our regional cuisine to the whole country."

Top:
"Frites," a popular tradition in northern Europe.

Above:
Production at a micro-brewery.

Facing page:
Mussels come from beds in the Baie de Somme or Mont Saint Michel (recipe page 195).

SERVES 4
- 6 oz shrimps
- ¼ bunch chives, chopped
- 4 large fresh free-range eggs
- 3 tablespoons crème fraîche
- 3 tablespoons lightly salted butter & 1 tablespoon for greasing the ramekins
- Salt, pepper

PREPARATION TIME
35 minutes

COOKING TIME
10 minutes

Eggs en Cocotte with Shrimps

Preheat oven to 325°F (170°C).

Wash and chop the chives. Carefully shell three-quarters of the shrimps (if not pre-shelled).

Butter 4 porcelain ramekins. Divide the shrimps between the ramekins and sprinkle with the chives. Break 1 egg into each of the ramekins, cover with the crème fraîche. Place the ramekins in a pan of hot water. Place directly on the gas for 1 minute and then put in the oven for 5 to 6 minutes.

When the eggs are cooked but still soft, remove from oven and garnish with the remaining shrimps and the chives.

Season to taste and serve immediately with large slices of buttered bread.

SERVES 8
- 12 oz ready-to-bake puff or regular pastry
- 1 lb ripened Maroilles cheese
- 5 eggs
- 4 tablespoons crème fraîche
- Nutmeg, grated
- ½ to 1 cup dark beer
- Salt, pepper

PREPARATION TIME
20 minutes

COOKING TIME
35 minutes

Maroilles Cheese Pie

Preheat oven to 400°F (200°C).

Roll out the pastry and line a 10-inch (24 cm) pie plate with it.

Remove the rind from the cheese, cut in large slices, and arrange evenly over the uncooked pie crust.

Beat the eggs with the cream, salt, pepper, and grated nutmeg. Add the beer, beating continuously, and pour over the cheese.

Bake the flan for 30 to 35 minutes. Serve hot accompanied by an arugula salad.

Classic French Fries with Sea Salt

Peel and rinse the potatoes, wipe dry in a cloth, and cut into even sticks about ⅓-inch (1 cm) in diameter and 4 inches (10 cm) long.

In a deep-fat fryer, heat the oil to 300°F (150°C).

Drop the potatoes into the hot oil. Cook for 10 minutes, stirring gently with a slotted spoon. The potatoes are cooked when they can be crushed between the fingers.

Drain the cooked potatoes on a clean cloth or absorbant paper.

Reheat the oil to 350° (180°C), drop the potatoes into the hot oil a second time, and cook until golden.

Drain on paper and season with coarse sea salt, stirring to distribute the salt evenly over the potatoes.

French-fried potatoes should be served crusty and hot, either alone or with mussels.

SERVES 4
- 8 large potatoes
- 8 cups sunflower oil
- 3 tablespoons coarse sea salt

PREPARATION TIME
30 minutes

COOKING TIME
30 minutes

Moules Marinière

Rinse the parsley, pare and wash the celery. Coarsely chop the parsley and celery.

Peel and chop the shallots. Crush the unpeeled garlic clove. Rinse and scrape the mussels.

Melt the butter in a large flameproof casserole, and add the shallots, garlic clove, chopped parsley and celery.

Cook over low heat for 2 minutes, then add the mussels. Shake the pot vigorously.

Add the white wine and cook over high heat for 8 to 10 minutes, stirring often.

When the mussels open, remove from heat, season to taste, and serve in large soup plates with some of the cooking liquid.

Serve in the Belgian style, with French fries.

SERVES 4
- 3 quarts (3 litres) mussels
- ½ bunch parsley
- 2 ribs celery
- 4 shallots
- 1 clove garlic
- 3 tablespoons lightly salted butter
- 2 cups white wine
- Salt, pepper

PREPARATION TIME
20 minutes

COOKING TIME
20 minutes

SERVES 4
- 2 carrots
- 2 leeks
- ½ celery root
- 2 shallots
- 1 large fillet of angler fish, cut into 8 slices
- 8 large prawns, shelled
- 2 cups white wine
- 2 tablespoons butter
- 1 lb mussels
- 1 cup fish stock
- 2 tablespoons crème fraîche
- 4 egg yolks
- 1 lemon
- Salt, pepper

PREPARATION TIME
35 minutes

COOKING TIME
35 minutes

The red brick and painted shutters typical of northern Europe.

Marmite Touquetoise

Preheat oven to 425°F (220°C).

Peel and wash the vegetables. Cut the carrots, leeks, and celery root into julienne strips.

Chop the shallots. Butter a large porcelain baking dish and scatter the chopped shallots over the bottom. Season with salt and pepper, add the pieces of angler fish and the prawns. Cover with the white wine and 2 cups of water. Bake for 10 minutes.

Melt 2 tablespoons of butter in a saucepan. Add the julienne vegetables and cook over low heat for 5 minutes, stirring constantly. Do not allow to color. Remove from heat, set aside, and keep warm.

Increase oven heat to 475°F (250°C).

Wash and scrape the mussels, add them to the ingredients in the baking dish. Cover with the fish stock and bake for another 10 minutes.

Meanwhile, beat the cream and egg yolks together in a bowl.

Remove the fish from the oven. Place the pieces of angler fish, the prawns, and the mussels in large soup plates. Pour the boiling cooking liquid from the pan over the julienne vegetables, add the cream-and-egg mixture, and whisk until the sauce has thickened. Correct the seasoning. Cover the contents of the soup plates with the sauce.

Steamed potatoes are a good accompaniment for this dish.

SERVES 8
- ½ cup milk
- 1 tablespoon yeast
- 1 pinch sugar
- ½ teaspoon salt
- 1 cup flour
- 4 tablespoons butter
- 2 eggs
- Cinnamon
- ½ cup brown sugar

PREPARATION TIME
30 minutes

WAITING TIME
1 hour 30 minutes

COOKING TIME
20 minutes

Traditional small shops continue to thrive.

Brown-Sugar Pie

Heat the milk to lukewarm and pour into a bowl. Add the yeast, sugar, and salt. Using the hands, mix these ingredients together thoroughly. Continue to mix while adding one egg and 4/5 of a cup of flour, sprinkling the flour lightly into the bowl. Cut the butter into small pieces and add gradually to the dough while continuing to mix.

Knead the dough vigorously, adding the remaining 1/5 cup flour. Form the dough into a ball and work with the hands until it is smooth and elastic.

Place the ball of dough on a plate, cover with a damp cloth, and allow to rise at room temperature for 1 hour or until double in bulk.

Sprinkle flour over a flat surface, roll out the dough, and line a greased pie-plate with it. Press the edges of the dough firmly around the edge of the pie-plate, cover with a damp cloth and allow to rise for another 30 minutes.

Preheat oven to 400°F (200°C).

In a bowl, mix a whole egg with a pinch of cinnamon, and spread over the pie shell. Sprinkle brown sugar over the whole surface of the egg glaze, and dot with knobs of butter. Bake for 20 minutes. Serve warm or cold.

MICHEL PORTOS

LE SAINT JAMES

BOULIAC

THE MAN

There are some things you just can't fight. When Michel Portos was about fifteen or sixteen, he suddenly developed a passion for cooking. He'd spend whole Saturdays haunting the culinary and gastronomy sections in local libraries. He knew he was destined to be a chef someday, but the parents of this dutiful son hadn't gotten the message. "Graduate from high school," they told him. "Go to college. Study for a real career."

"After my first year majoring in accounting, I quit and passed my CAP diploma in cooking. My father had a fit. My decision caused a major upheaval in our family." It was a decision based on high ambitions, however. This young man from Marseilles wasn't interested in pizza or fast food. The path he chose would lead him, ultimately, into the ranks of truly great chefs. "At the time, I spent every penny I made—and I didn't make many—on restaurant meals. I never set foot in a nightclub. I saved everything I could so that, once or twice a year, I could take my girlfriend to dinner in a top restaurant. I needed to educate my palate, to acquire a whole culture, a sort of personal dictionary."

It was a matter of character. Michel Portos aimed high. He wanted to work with the best products, deal with the best caviar, slice the most delicate foie gras. "I had then, and still have now, a taste for luxury and the best of everything. A fascination, for example, for the people awarded the "Meilleur Ouvrier de France" title. These are people with an obsession; people willing to spend hours perfecting a single dish, attending to the smallest details. And all this despite the fact that their work is, by definition, ephemeral."

Michel Portos followed the same path, but in his own way. It was a path that inevitably led him to the best restaurants. To Dominique Toulouzy's Jardins de l'Opéra, Michel Trama's L'Aubergade, and a stint with the Troigros brothers, who are now his close friends. He next settled in Perpignan, where he finally opened his own restaurant.

Left to right:
A plate of shallots.
Doudou, the Saint James
wine steward.
Boning pigeons.

Facing page:
Jean Nouvel's architecture stands
out against the traditional
village church.

Following double page:
Juice from celery ribs and green
apples put through
the food processor.
Will it work . . . or not?
Developing a new recipe
mobilizes the entire team.

Six tables, a staff of two in the kitchen, and a first star awarded after only two years by the Michelin Guide. "That's when I knew I was on the right track."

Meanwhile, he also recognized the limitations of his situation. If he wanted to make progress, he'd have to have a whole team behind him, giving him the means to develop recipes that interested him, the time to try out new dishes. That's when he landed at Le Saint James, where he replaced Jean-Marie Amat.

THE REGION

The site is very special: an old country manor once used by Bordeaux's elite as a hideaway for romantic trysts. The house itself is more than a building; it's a work of art. A counterpoint of glass and old ironwork on the façade, intriguing nooks and crannies in the bedrooms, partial views of a vineyard, the Garonne River, and the town, framed by the dining room's geometric bay windows. Here, there is a blend of luxury and natural materials, unfinished cement and polished plaster, forming a splash of incongruity in the still waters of French country inns and château-hotels.

This imposing and historic spot had received the attention of a leading architect, Jean Nouvel, who had been commissioned by the former owner, Jean-Marie Amat, a talented chef and native of the region. The two men's revolutionary ideas, plus their desire to create a different kind of hotel would appeal to artists and esthetes, made waves in the conventional French hotel industry of the time. Much water has flowed over the dam since then. Jean-Marie Amat eventually lost control of his own business, and Michel Portos was asked to replace him.

The problem for Portos was whether or not to accept to confront the ghost of this hotel-restaurant's founder, or turn his back on the challenge. "It was a real dilemma. I mulled it over for a long time, I asked other chefs for advice. And then I decided to risk it." This was partly because Nouvel's understated architecture, although commissioned by another man, suits the decidedly Asian understatement of Portos's cuisine.

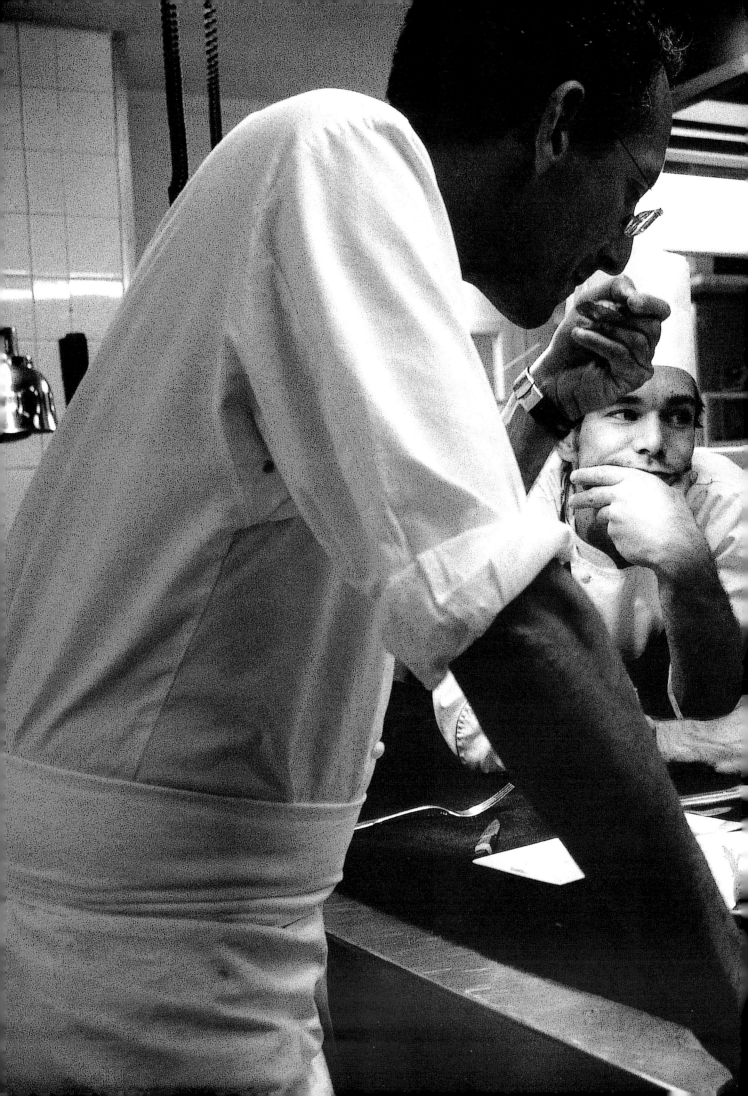

Partly because, in a word, there was still so much to do. But it was mainly, despite the house's reverses of fortune, to confirm an intuition of Amat's: that Le Saint James, with its extraordinary décor, has everything it takes to become a great institution, to survive the men who first created it. The facilities that Michel Portos now has at his command—the kitchen and its skilled staff—are commensurate with his talent.

THE STYLE

Don't count on Portos for Bordelaise-style lampreys or rib steak grilled over grapevine twigs. There are excellent restaurants in town that specialize in these regional standards. On the other hand, the cuisine of this man, exiled from Marseilles to the Bordelais, is not totally out of place here. Olive oil from Provence combines naturally with foie gras; mushrooms and truffles make their proper appearance in season; meagre—a fish native to the Gironde River—goes well with Jerusalem artichokes; oysters straight from the cove at Arcachon are served with Andalusian pomegranates.

Michel Portos invents dishes that telescope geography. Soy-sauce reductions, or a hint of ginger or grilled sesame-seed oil are occasional reminders that he once traveled to Japan. "I like to keep things simple. I've cleared my tables of everything extraneous, even salt and pepper shakers."

Many of the dishes on Portos' menu list the names of friends and neighbors who supply the raw materials. The wood strawberries served on a crisp pastry shell come from Madame Loubière, the squab is from Monsieur Hazera in Camarsac. And the caviar comes, of course, from the Gironde River. "It's really true, you know. There have always been sturgeon in the Gironde, and over the past ten years or so our producers have made enormous progress." Portos is open-minded, and eager to put down roots in his new home. The first thing he did on his arrival in Bouliac was to ask the Chamber of Commerce for a list of local suppliers.

The cellars of Le Saint James are currently being brought up to speed. They contain just as many grands crus and premiers crus as ever—they have to, in this region—but now include wines from other regions as well. There are now wines from Languedoc, Provence, Burgundy, even Spain. "I enjoy working with wine stewards. And sometimes I'm the one who chooses the wine, because I'm the one who knows what's most suitable for my dishes. Here as elsewhere, I'm flexible. I just try to cast a fresh eye on local products and gastronomy."

Top to bottom:
*Aquitaine caviar, an old
tradition revisited.
Fishermen's cabins
on the Garonne.
The impeccable taste
of wine steward Doudou.*

Facing page:
*Although originally from
Marseilles, Michel Portos knows
how to select the best products
offered by the Bordelais region.*

Japanese-Style Squab

SERVES 4
- 4 squabs
- 8 oz Japanese noodles
- 1 cup chicken stock
- 4 raw shrimp
- 12 peeled lemon wedges
- 2 teaspoons wasabi
- 5 tablespoons soy sauce
- 3 tablespoons grilled peanut oil
- Fresh mixed herbs

PREPARATION TIME
35 minutes

COOKING TIME
35 minutes

Preheat oven to 375°F (190°C).

Oven-roast the squab for 20 minutes.

Cook the noodles in the chicken stock.

Arrange the noodles in a large soup plate, top with the shrimp and lemon wedges.

Mix the wasabi with the soy sauce and grilled-peanut oil.

Pour this sauce and the chicken stock over the noodles.

Bone the squabs and arrange the breasts and thighs on the bed of noodles.

Garnish with the fresh mixed herbs.

Oysters with Herb Butter

SERVES 4
- 20 oysters
- 1 cucumber
- 1 pomegranate
- 1 bunch flat parsley
- 3 tablespoons soy sauce
- 2 tablespoons lemon juice
- 1 clove garlic, chopped
- 8 tablespoons butter

PREPARATION TIME
25 minutes

COOKING TIME
8 minutes

Open the oysters, drain on a cloth, set the shells aside.

Peel the cucumber and cut into thin julienne strips.

Cut the pomegranate in two and remove the seeds. Wash, stem, and chop the parsley.

Mix together the soy sauce, lemon juice, and chopped garlic.

Fill the oyster shells with the julienne strips of cucumber and top with an oyster.

Heat the butter in a saucepan until it turns light brown. Add the soy sauce mixture, pomegranate seeds, and chopped parsley.

Pour a generous tablespoon of this herb butter over each oyster.

Page 210:
Oysters and pomegranates—a novel blend of flavors.

Page 211:
The tranquility of the Arcachon cove.

SERVES 8

For the pastry cream
- 3 egg yolks
- 3 tablespoons sugar
- 2 tablespoons flour
- 1 cup milk
- 1 vanilla pod
- 2 tablespoons butter
- 1 tablespoon dried lavender

For the chiffon cream
- 1 sheet gelatin
- Pastry cream (see above)
- ½ cup heavy cream, whipped

For the licorice "spoom"
- 1 cup sugar
- 4 cups water
- 1 tablespoon licorice drops
- 2 sheets gelatin

For the fig chips
- 8 firm figs
- Sugar for dredging
- Butter for greasing

For the baked figs
- 8 ripe figs
- 1 oz butter
- Granulated sugar for dredging
- Dash of balsamic vinegar

For the fig tartare
- 8 ripe figs
- 1 tablespoon lemon juice

PREPARATION TIME
1 hour 30 minutes

COOKING TIME
45 minutes

Elegance drawing on both the old and the new.

Three Reasons to Love Figs

- *Preparing the pastry cream*: Beat the egg yolks, sugar, and flour together until well blended. Scald the milk and simmer for 3 minutes with a vanilla pod for taste. Soften the gelatin in a bowl of cold water. Remove the milk from heat, blend with the egg-yolk mixture, add the butter, lavender and the gelatin. Set aside.

- *Preparing the chiffon cream*: Mix the pastry cream and whipped cream, blending thoroughly.

- *Preparing the licorice "spoom"*: Make a syrup with the sugar and water. Add the licorice drops and softened gelatin. Fill a chantilly "bombe" with this mixture, adjust the gas canisters, and place in a cool spot.

- *Preparing the fig chips*: Preheat oven to 350°F (180°C). Butter a baking sheet and dredge with sugar. Cut the figs into thin slices and place on the baking sheet. Bake until the slices have dried out.

- *Preparing the baked figs*: Preheat oven to 350°F (180°C). Cut a cross into the upper half of each fig. Fill the opening with a dab of butter and dredge the figs in granulated sugar. Sprinkle with a little balsamic vinegar and bake 5 minutes.

- *Preparing the fig tartare*: Shred the figs and mix with a little lemon juice.

- *Fifteen minutes before serving*: In the middle of a plate, arrange 1 baked fig beside a mound of fig tartare. Garnish with the licorice "spoom." Decorate the edges of the plate with the fig chips and lavender pastry cream.

SERVES 8

For the pastry cream
- 2 egg yolks
- 4 tablespoons sugar
- 2 tablespoons flour
- 1 vanilla pod
- 1 cup milk
- 2 tablespoons butter

For the soufflé
- 4 fresh egg whites
- 5 tablespoons sugar
- Pastry cream (see above)
- 3 tablespoons lemon juice
- 20 drops tangerine extract

PREPARATION TIME
40 minutes

COOKING TIME
25 minutes

Tangerine Soufflé

- *Preparing the pastry cream*: Beat the egg yolks, sugar, and flour together until well blended. Split the vanilla pod, scrape the seeds into the milk and add the husk. Scald the milk and simmer for 3 minutes. Remove from heat, blend thoroughly with the egg-yolk mixture, and add the butter. Set aside.
- *Preparing the soufflé*: Preheat oven to 350°F (180°C). Whip the egg whites until firm, adding the sugar gradually. Add the warm pastry cream, lemon juice, and tangerine extract. Using a rubber spatula, gently fold and stir until blended.

Butter individual molds (or cups) and dredge with sugar. Fill with the soufflé mixture and bake 20 minutes.

SERVES 4
(makes 16 macaroons)

For the macaroons
- 1 tablespoon fresh egg whites
- ½ cup stale egg whites
- 3 tablespoons pulverized almonds
- ½ cup confectioners' sugar

For the pistachio cream
- 1 tablespoon raw almond paste
- 1 teaspoon pistachio paste
- ½ tablespoon butter
- 1 teaspoon kirsch
- ½ teaspoon heavy cream

PREPARATION TIME
1 hour

COOKING TIME
20 minutes

Pistachio Macaroons

- *Preparing the macaroons*: Whip all the egg whites until stiff. Using a rubber spatula, gently fold in the pulverized almonds and confectioners' sugar.

Cover a baking sheet with ovenproof paper. Fill a pastry bag (No. 8) with the macaroon dough and press small disks onto the baking sheet. Allow to rest for 30 minutes. Preheat oven to 350°F (180°C).

Bake the macaroons for 10 minutes.

- *Preparing the pistachio cream*: Thoroughly blend the almond and pistachio pastes. Add the melted butter, kirsch, and cream.

Gently detach the macaroons from the baking sheet. Taking two macaroons at a time, spread the pistachio cream on the flat side of one of them, then sandwich it together against the flat side of the other macaroon.

OLIVIER ROELLINGER

THE MAN

On his way to being a chemist, Olivier Roellinger turned into an alchemist. As the dutiful son of a country doctor, he took advanced courses in math and science for a degree in engineering. Then he suddenly decided to try for a CAP diploma in cooking, passed the exam, apprenticed with some of the greatest names in the field, and returned home five weeks later. That's when he set off for his own Treasure Island, his isle of heady fragrances.

At first he set his sights on a modest country inn, but in no time he'd joined the ranks of his generation's most inspired chefs. He fought valiantly against the trend for neo-luxury ghettoes, installing his restaurant's kitchen and dining room in his old childhood home, a granite manor house typical of the Saint-Malo region. His mother still lives upstairs. Some of his guests retire after dinner to a small cliff-side cottage his wife fell in love with. The others stay at the Château de Bricart, a manor that, when Roellinger was a boy, was said to be haunted, and the place where Léon Blum spent country holidays. Roellinger's world has expanded, but it is structured. It reflects the consistency of his own ideas.

When Olivier Roellinger was a teenager, he believed in "reason," a conviction sorely tested by an ordeal that perhaps explains his abrupt shift from engineering to cuisine. One day, at the foot of the Saint-Malo ramparts and with no apparent motive, he was attacked and severely beaten. He lay in a coma for a week, and afterward spent more than a year in a wheelchair. It was an experience that changed his view of life for ever. Also, when he was only twelve, his father abandoned the family. "When that happened, maybe I decided to make my life an extension of my childhood." And so, today, he entertains guests the way his parents did, when they were still a united couple.

Olivier Roellinger draws on the countryside when creating his dishes, citing such sources of inspiration as the region's typical granite stone, visible at every turn in the road, and the apple orchards and cider, characteristic of Celtic countries everywhere. To all of this is added the Bay of Mont-Saint-Michel, his beacon on the horizon. "It's like the pulse of the universe, shifting sands moving in rhythm with the moon. Some ten billion cubic feet of water rolling in each day. At low tide, you walk on the seabed."

Saint-Malo rises across the bay like Quebec, Cape Horn, the Indies or San Francisco. It is a port facing other shores, other suns. Olivier Roellinger once found some china plates from the East India Company in his own house. He had copies made, and uses the new set for presenting his "Maritime Adventures" menu. When the tide comes in, he thinks of seafarers journeying to the ends of the earth. The ocean spray brings with it a hint of Valparaiso, the fragrance of cinnamon, and the tang of ginger. Just like his restaurant.

THE REGION

Oysters. Here, they're given the respect usually reserved for vintage wines. Twice daily, at low tide, the oyster beds at the foot of the Cancale cliffs emerge from the water. They're owned by some forty oystermen. Roellinger knows them all, but always buys from the same one. "Look at this bottle of Puligny-Montrachet. It's a great wine, but there are variations from vineyard to vineyard. It's the same for oysters. The flavor of an oyster depends on how fast the tide comes in and out, how much soft water flows over it. The way individual oystermen work accentuates the differences." Olivier Roellinger could talk about oysters forever. He serves them as they are, or slightly heated, "warm as a baby's hand." He likes to see those rough, primitive shells gracing an elegant table. Because oysters are one of the few foods eaten live, and because their energy is concentrated, a single mouthful contains the entire power of the sea.

The sea is Olivier Roellinger's element. The impact of his cuisine comes from the sea: oysters from beds in the bay; sole, shrimp, and squid in season; deep-sea bass; lobsters caught by a man who knew Roellinger's grandfather; sea grass, sea chard, a touch of seaweed—vegetables from sea and cliff.

Roellinger claims to have only one true family: the chefs; the people who, whether French, Australian, or Indian, work with a vegetable patch behind them and their eyes fixed on distant horizons. His own vegetable patch is a fine one, with artichokes, onions, strawberries, and cabbage. Charlotte potatoes and carrots are rooted in the sand. Olivier Roellinger knows the fields around him. He's seen his elders spread kelp on the furrows of plowed soil to fertilize it. He's learned that, in this spot, the land owes a debt to the sea.

Facing page:
The typically blue
Brittany lobster.

Orders posted in the kitchen.

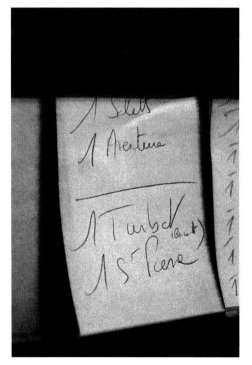

A true Breton, he's propelled by winds from the four corners of the globe. He claims that French cuisine was at its most robust during the twelfth century, when it adopted the potatoes, corn, and beans from America. He points out that France would never have known the Plougastel strawberry if the seedlings hadn't been first imported from Chile. His conclusion: French cuisine is many things to many people, but it should not be an eco-museum.

THE STYLE

Vertical. Olivier Roellinger describes his style as vertical, not a word often associated with gastronomy. This reflects his maritime attitude. The only reliable beacons for a ship at sea are vertical ones: the mast, a lighthouse etched against the horizon. Roellinger's horizon, when he creates a dish, is the plate. Against the white china, he raises a vertical beacon of scallops beside an artichoke heart and sliver of apple. He draws slender lines of spice and sauce, builds up layers of flavor and texture. Verticality is his life; is life itself.

The composition will be destroyed by the fork, of course. On the other hand, because the fork mixes the separate flavors together, it encourages experimentation. Roellinger's maître d'hôtel occasionally confides a few little secrets, such as the proper sequence to follow in order to develop the palate. The dash of licorice-flavored marshmallow should be added as a final touch—at the end, and only at the end—to the lobster dubbed "Sailing Home from the Indies." Sea-bass fillets receive a dash of tangy vinegar; raw shelled shrimp are marinated in aged malt whisky. Diners at Roellinger's table will perceive the occasional hint of poppy, sesame, candied grapefruit, or angelica peel. But there's no time to linger on these evocations of distant lands. The chef has already moved on.

There's never been food like this. Are we at the beginning of the meal or the end? Is this the appetizer or the main dish? And yet, everything retains its distinctive flavor. Roellinger's cuisine skips from ocean to ocean, piles continent upon continent, but it

Preceding double page:
Mont Saint Michel towers over the bay.

A discussion conducted by the seaside in front of Les Rimains, Olivier Roellinger's first hotel.

Facing page:
Butter—lightly salted, of course.

is never eccentric. It shows a subtle respect for our own standards and memories. It's original but familiar: this is the source of its strength.

You'll find Roellinger in the kitchen. He's on hand at each service, and not just to approve the dishes as they leave for the dining room. With his blue apron wrapped around his waist, he darts back and forth in front of his counter, waiting for orders, checking on his pots and pans, tasting and re-tasting. His staff bustle around him, moving quickly and surely in concentrated silence. There are no wasted gestures, no loud words. Roellinger can't stand people who yell. One of his assistants, who is Japanese, brushes black cakes with oil and arranges them by threes on a plate. Such are the mysteries of Roellinger's craft. Another, as if he had all the time in the world, carefully measures minuscule bits of pastry with a schoolroom ruler. Only Roellinger understands everything that's going on, as only a creator can. A creator who never writes his recipes down and is not particularly interested in technique. A man who enjoys the sound of fish sizzling in the oven. A sensual spirit.

Far left:
The restaurant is housed in the family's former residence.

Left:
Periwinkles served at apéritif time.

Facing page:
André Hélan, a faithful assistant from the earliest days who earned his CAP diploma with Olivier Roellinger. The man in charge of cooking the lobsters.

SERVES 4
- 2 Brittany lobsters
  (1½ lb each)
- 5 oz salted butter
- ⅓ cup sherry
- ½ vanilla pod
- 10 annatto seeds
- 1 unwaxed lemon
- 1 tablespoon coriander seeds
- 1 cup chicken stock

PREPARATION TIME
40 minutes

COOKING TIME
20 minutes

The Bay of Cancale.

Lobster "Petit Pagaille" with Sherry and Lemon Zest

Drop the lobsters into boiling water and cook for 2 minutes.

Remove the heads and claws. Cut the heads open with kitchen shears and remove the sand pouch. Crush the head shells.

Sauté the crushed head shells in the salted butter, add the sherry, reduce by one-half. Add the vanilla pod, annatto seeds, juice of 1 lemon, and coriander seeds.

Cover with chicken stock. Simmer until reduced by one-third. Press through a conical purée strainer while shaking the strainer vigorously.

Remove the lobster meat from body and claws, setting aside the juice from the shells.

In a large frying pan, sauté the pieces of lobster meat briefly in butter. Cook until the meat is translucent, but do not allow to color. Remove from heat and deglaze with the juice from the lobster shells.

Serve the tail and claw meat on warm plates, covered with the smooth, strained sauce.

SERVES 12
- 4 oz cow's-milk yogurt
- 2 lb scallops (without the coral)
- 5 tablespoons sea salt
- 1 lb lamb's lettuce
- ¼ bunch chives, chopped
- Paprika
- Fleur de sel

For the oriental-spice mixture
- Grated nutmeg
- 2 tablespoons ground coriander
- 2 tablespoons ground cumin
- 1 teaspoon black pepper
- 2 tablespoons green anise

For the marinade
- 1 cup water
- 5 tablespoons sugar
- ¾ cup lemon juice
- 2 cups distilled vinegar

For the vinaigrette
- ½ cup passion-fruit juice
- 1 cup pineapple juice
- Cayenne pepper
- Saffron
- 1 cups peanut oil
- ½ cup almond oil
- Salt, pepper

PREPARATION TIME
1 hour

COOKING TIME
- Yogurt steeping, 8 hours
- Salt marinade, 3 hours
- Vinaigrette marinade, 2 hours

The redecoration of the hotel's bed-rooms was personally supervised by Roellinger.

Scallops with Oriental Spices

Stir 2 tablespoons of the oriental-spice mixture into the yogurt. Steep for 8 hours. Strain.

Cover the scallops with the sea salt, set aside for 3 hours. Rinse the scallops and soak for 1 hour in cold water to remove all traces of salt.

Drain and rinse the scallops, then place in the marinade and steep for 10 minutes.

Finally, transfer the scallops to the vinaigrette and chill for 2 hours.

Cut the scallops into thin round slices about ⅛-inch (3 mm) thick. On large plates, arrange alternating rows of the sliced scallops and spiced yogurt.

Garnish with the lettuce and chives. Season with fleur de sel.

Kouign Amann

In a large bowl, use the fingertips to combine the dry ingredients for the pastry dough until thoroughly blended. Add the milk and water, blend until smooth, and then knead vigorously for 5 minutes. Form the dough into a ball, place in bowl, cover with a damp cloth and allow to rise for 45 minutes at room temperature.

Meanwhile, for the butter mixture, carefully blend the creamed butter, sugar, and flour in another bowl. Shape this mixture into an even square measuring about 6 × 6 inches (15 × 15 cm).

When the pastry dough has risen to about twice its original bulk, use a rolling pin to shape it into a large square double the size of the butter square. Place the butter square on top of the pastry square. Fold the edges of the pastry square over the butter square, left-to-right and right-to-left, so they overlap. Roll this "dough package" into a strip measuring about 30 inches (80 cm) long by 8 inches (15-20 cm) wide. Again fold the dough in three so that it overlaps. Allow to rest for 20 minutes in the refrigerator. Turn the pastry band so that the open edges are in front of you. Repeat the rolling, folding, turning, and resting process three times. This is called "making 3 turns."

Preheat oven to 325°F (160°C).

Sprinkle your work counter with the 5 tablespoons of sugar. Roll the dough out on the sugar, forming a large square about 1/5-inch (½ cm) thick. Cut the pastry dough into a large circle and place sugar-side down in a rimmed metal pie-pan.

Bake the Kouign Amann for 45 minutes. When it is cooked and golden, remove from oven, turn it over in the pan, and allow to cool a little at room temperature.

Best when served warm.

SERVES 6-8

For the pastry dough
- 2 cups flour
- 1 teaspoon salt
- 1 tablespoon melted butter
- 1 tablespoon sugar
- 1 tablespoon yeast
- ½ cup milk
- 1 cup water

For the butter mixture
- 2 cups lightly salted butter, creamed until soft
- 1 cup sugar & 5 tablespoons for rolling out the dough
- ½ cup flour

PREPARATION TIME
1 hour

COOKING TIME
45 minutes

Page 232:
All roads lead to the sea.

Page 233:
Lemon-flavored olive oil.

SERVES 4

For the pineapple mousse
• 1 pineapple
• 2 sheets gelatin
• 1 cup caster sugar
• ½ cinnamon stick

For the rum and cider grog
• 4 cups cider
• 1 cup brown sugar
• ½ cup granulated sugar
• ½ cinnamon stick
• 1 vanilla pod
• 1 clove
• 1 nutmeg
• Fresh ginger
• Zest of 2 limes

For the coconut caramel
• 1 cup sugar
• 2 cups coconut milk
• Juice of 1 lime

• ½ lb puff pastry
• 1 mango
• 4 passion fruit
• 2 bananas
• Butter for sautéeing
• 1 tablespoon grated coconut
• 4 sprigs lemon balm
• Juice of 2 limes
• 1 cup "Marie-Galante" rum

Dreaming of faraway places.

PREPARATION TIME
2 hours

STEEPING TIME
2 hours

COOKING TIME
45 minutes

An Invitation to Exotic Lands: Pineapple Millefeuille with Rum and Cider Grog

• *Preparing the pineapple mousse*: Soften the sheets of gelatin in cold water.

Cut the pineapple into 8 sections and remove the tough inner core. Set aside one section and cut the other seven into small strips.

Place 4 cups water, 1 cup sugar, and ½ of the cinnamon stick in a pot. Bring to a boil, add the strips of pineapple, simmer 20 minutes. Mix in blender. Add the softened sheets of gelatin and chill.

• *Preparing the grog*: In a large pot mix together 6 cups water, 4 cups cider, 1 cup brown sugar, ½ cup granulated sugar, ½ of the cinnamon stick, 1 vanilla pod (split lengthwise and scraped), 1 clove, 1 nutmeg (crushed), 1 tablespoon grated fresh ginger, and the zest from 2 limes. Bring to a boil, remove from heat and allow to steep 2 hours. Strain.

• *Preparing the coconut caramel*: Heat 1 cup sugar over low heat, stirring constantly with wooden spoon. When the sugar melts and turns a light caramel color, add 2 cups coconut milk and the juice of 1 lime. Simmer until the caramel has melted and the mixture is smooth and thoroughly blended. Set aside.

Preheat oven to 350°F (180°C).

Roll the puff pastry into a thin, ⅛-inch (2 mm) rectangle measuring about 10 × 15 inches (20 × 30 cm) in area. Place on baking sheet and bake approximately 15 minutes, until golden. Cool. Using a ruler and a pastry cutter, divide into smaller rectangles measuring 1½ × ½ inch (6 x 1½ cm).

Peel the mango and the remaining section of pineapple and cut into cubes. Add the passion-fruit seeds and pulp.

Slice the bananas and sauté lightly in butter. Deglaze with the coconut caramel mixture. Lightly grill the shredded coconut.

To serve, divide the millefeuille rectangles into four equal stacks and transfer the stacks to dessert plates. Use a pastry bag to spread the pineapple mousse between each layer of millefeuille. Pile a mound of warm bananas on one side of the plates. Garnish with the grilled grated coconut, decorate with a sprig of lemon balm.

Heat the grog. At the last moment, add the juice of 2 limes and the "Marie Galante" rum. Serve the grog in mugs garnished with 2 tablespoons of the cubed fruit.

MATHIEU VIANNAY

CHEZ MATHIEU VIANNAY

LYON

THE MAN

The usual practice is for chefs to open bistros only after their reputation has been established. On the Place des Brotteaux, for example, Georges Blanc opened his brasserie opposite the one inaugurated by Paul Bocuse in a former railroad station. Mathieu Viannay decided to do things differently. As an unknown newcomer, he chose not to apprentice with some famous chef, but immediately acquired an old bar on an avenue in a good Lyon neighborhood and converted it into a little bistro. Baptizing his new acquisition "Les Oliviers," he proved a devoted apostle of quality Provençal cuisine. As the new bistro filled with satisfied customers, its chef began to make a name for himself. In 2001 he felt confident enough to aim higher. And so, next door to Les Oliviers, he opened another restaurant, this time without any regional affiliation. He called it "Chez Mathieu Viannay," thus putting his name on the line and indicating that the cuisine would have a more personal touch—which it does.

This young man, who was born in Versailles, grew up in Paris, and moved to Lyon to oversee the kitchen at the Part-Dieu railroad station, progressed gradually. At the age of thirty-three he won the acceptance of his peers through Bocuse, who dined at the new restaurant three days after it opened—and gave it his blessing. Meanwhile, Bocuse also lent Mathieu his interior designer, Vavro, the man responsible for the décor of the Monsieur Paul brasseries. The main staircase leading to the mezzanine was Vavro's idea, as was the combination of white stone and colored lighting fixtures, a pared-down rococo setting with a touch of stylish modernity. "People in Lyon who aren't used to this kind of thing feel almost as though they're slumming when they come here. As if they were having dinner in a nightclub."

Mathieu Viannay carefully studied the other restaurants in Lyon, learning what he did and didn't want for his own. He didn't want the kind of ceremonial décor recalling the starchy formal banquets of his childhood. He didn't want a stiff upper-class

Left to right:
A quick snack for the busy chef.
Saint Jean cathedral.
A visit from Georges, a friend
who is both a wine steward and
a specialist in rare wines.

Facing page:
Fruit soup (recipe page 250).

Following double spread:
Preparation of foie gras sautéed
with candied lemon.

atmosphere inappropriate to the pace of contemporary life. And most of all, he didn't want any gilded youths with a sense of inbred entitlement. "I've always believed in keeping my prices low. I can't stand the thought of an empty restaurant. The main thing is to have a full house. Putting a personal stamp on it comes afterward."

Time is on his side. His dining room is full to bursting, noon and night. Full of guests who aren't yet willing to spend astronomical sums of money. They don't really know him that well. Their top priority is value-for-money. To help them get acquainted, he enhances every dish with those little extras straight from the heart that, in the long run, identify a chef as the kind of artist for whom people throw caution to the winds.

THE REGION

Mathieu Viannay's wine list features some sixty different Côtes-du-Rhône but only a few Beaujolais vintages. The latter are there for the sake of form and to satisfy people who simply must have them. In Lyon, this tells you something.

In a city midway between North and South, Viannay has decided to set his course down the great river, toward the Mediterranean. Not that he specializes in Provençal cuisine. He doesn't feel attached to any particular region and refuses to obey the dictates of either Aix or Lyon. However, his own taste requires the use of olive oil rather than cream, and he cooks fish from the South more often than chicken from Bresse. "Furthermore, if I feel like using soy sauce to heighten a particular flavor, I do it. Oriental products are also part of my repertoire, not because they're fashionable, but because they really interest me." Viannay belongs to the generation of chefs who have no boundaries.

Mathieu Viannay doesn't nourish any special manias when he does his marketing in Lyon, and he doesn't have any favorite suppliers, either. He just looks for the best. Although neither of his parents worked professionally in the field of cuisine (his father

was a fluid-mechanics engineer, his mother a relaxation therapist) they did teach him the basics. A taste for fine cheese, vegetables from the garden, and fish cooked when absolutely fresh. "The quality of the raw ingredients is crucial," concludes Mathieu Viannay, "But apart from quality, I'm no fanatic. For me, the difference comes from what the chef does with his materials."

THE STYLE

When you stop to think about it, you realize that all the dishes on Mathieu Viannay's menu are relatively simple. One of his tasting menus might feature pumpkin soup, sardines on a rectangle of pastry, braised veal with mashed potatoes, and madeleines for dessert. Basic—except at the same time everything is balanced, down to the tiniest detail. The pumpkin soup is garnished with a ladleful of whipped cream, seasoned with bacon and topped with a sliver of truffle: the crowning touch. The bed of tomatoes under the raw sardines has no hint of acidity. The mashed potatoes are smooth and velvety, and the madeleines—spiced with a few drops of truffle honey from Italy—are sublime. At this level, simplicity becomes a subtle art.

The banks of the Rhône at Lyon.

Facing page:
The dining room, decorated by interior designer Vavro, a friend of Bocuse's.

As a student at hotel school, Mathieu Viannay already had a reputation for the apparently effortless way he did things. He was always the first to finish his exam papers. To his classmates it looked as though he wasn't really trying and was set to take a fall. Viannay wasn't worried. He always passed with flying colors. He had what it takes: the gift, all the answers.

His style comes so naturally to him that he still finds it hard to analyze, even today. It is understated, with no frills. He does have a theory, though; one that fits him like a glove. As he explains: "To keep things simple, I never put more than three different components on a single plate. For meat or fish, I stick to just a little sauce and one garnish." His theory as applied to his menu gives us, for example, poached sausage with grilled bacon, split-pea purée, and truffle juice. That's it. Everything perfectly balanced. Mathieu doesn't need to gild the lily. His talent is best expressed through simplicity.

SERVES 4
• 24 fresh sardine fillets
• 1 lb ready-to-bake puff pastry
• 1 egg, beaten

For the basil oil
• 2 sprigs basil
• ½ cup olive oil

For the tomato sauce
• 6 ripe tomatoes
• 2 shallots
• 2 tablespoons butter
• 1 bouquet garni
• Salt, pepper
• ½ teaspoon sugar
• 4 fresh mint leaves

For the marinade
• 1 cup white wine
• ⅓ cup sherry vinegar
• Juice of 1 lemon
• 1 tablespoon acacia honey

PREPARATION TIME
40 minutes

COOKING TIME
40 minutes

In the kitchen.

Sardines in Pastry

• *Preparing the basil oil*: Rinse the basil, remove the leaves, and blend in a food processor with the olive oil. Season to taste and chill.
• *Preparing the tomato sauce*: Scald the tomatoes for 1 minute, drain, and refresh under cold water. With the tip of a paring knife, carefully peel the tomatoes, cut in two, remove seeds, and chop.

   Peel and chop the shallots. Melt the butter in a saucepan, add the chopped shallots, bouquet garni, and tomatoes. Season with salt, pepper, and ½ teaspoon sugar. Simmer for 20 minutes, stirring occasionally, until smooth and thick. Correct the seasoning, transfer to a bowl, and cool. Wash and chop the mint leaves, stir into the cooled tomatoes.
• *Preparing the marinade*: In a bowl, mix together the white wine, sherry vinegar, lemon juice, and honey. Season to taste and bring to scalding point over high heat. Set aside and keep hot.

Preheat oven to 350°F (175°C).

   Cut the puff pastry into 4 identical rectangles, brush with the beaten egg, and bake for 25 minutes. When the pastry is crusty and golden, remove from oven and allow to cool at room temperature.

   Arrange the sardine fillets skin-side up in a porcelain serving dish. Cover with the warm marinade and allow to cool at room temperature.

   Place a section of the cooked pastry on each plate, cover with the tomato sauce. Arrange 6 sardine fillets on the sauce. Season with fleur de sel, a little of the marinade, and the basil oil.

SERVES 4
- **16 prawns**
- **4 tablespoons grilled sesame seeds**
- **4 spring onions**
- **4 tablespoons butter**
- **1 tablespoon curry powder**
- **2 Rodrigue peppers**
- **¼ cup white wine**
- **½ cup coconut milk**
- **Salt, pepper**
- **3 gray shallots**
- **1½ cups "Arborio" rice for risotto**
- **2 cups hot chicken stock**
- **¼ cup crème fraîche**
- **¼ cup olive oil**
- **4 tablespoons peanut oil**

PREPARATION TIME
40 minutes

COOKING TIME
30 minutes

A team with a personal touch.

Curried Risotto with Prawns

Shell the prawns and dredge in the sesame seeds.

Peel the spring onions, cut off the green portion and set aside; chop the bulbs.

Melt the butter in a saucepan, add the chopped onion and the heads and shells of the prawns. Simmer for 3 minutes, stirring constantly. Add the curry powder and peppers, simmer 3 minutes longer. Add the white wine, reduce by one-half, add the coconut milk.

Season the sauce to taste with salt and simmer for 15 minutes, stirring occasionally. When the sauce is thick and smooth, strain and keep hot.

About 25 minutes before serving, peel and chop the gray shallots. Heat the olive oil in a large frying pan. Add the rice and shallots to the hot oil and cook over low heat for 4 minutes, stirring to burst the grains of rice. Moisten slightly with the hot chicken stock and simmer until the rice begins to expand. Repeat, gradually adding more stock, until the rice is fully cooked—tender but slightly firm. Add the crème fraîche, season to taste, stir.

Sauté the prawns briefly in the peanut oil. Serve the rice topped with curry sauce and garnished with the prawns and the chopped green portion of the onions.

SERVES 4
- 3 lb veal shoulder
- 4 tablespoons peanut oil
- 6 cups cold water
- 1 bouquet garni
- 1 large onion, studded with a clove
- 4 carrots
- 1 leek
- 2 lb salsify
- 2 tablespoons flour
- ¼ cup crème fraîche
- 2 tablespoons butter
- Salt, pepper
- 1 fresh truffle

PREPARATION TIME
45 minutes

COOKING TIME
3 hours

Braised Shoulder of Veal with Fresh Truffle

Heat the peanut oil in a large flameproof casserole, add the meat, brown, and season.

When the meat is browned on all sides, add 6 cups cold water. Reduce to simmer, add the bouquet garni, the onion studded with the clove, and the carrots and leek, washed and peeled. Simmer for 3 hours.

Pare and wash the salsify, cook until done in a pot of water mixed with the flour.

Drain and rinse the salsify, blend in a food processor with the crème fraîche and butter. Season to taste and keep warm.

Reduce the veal stock until syrupy, add 3 tablespoons butter, blend.

When the meat is spoon-tender, remove from pot, drain, and separate into 4 equal portions. Place mounds of salsify purée on each of four plates, top with a piece of veal, garnish with slices of fresh truffle. Pour the sauce over the meat just before serving.

SERVES 4
- ½ sheet gelatin
- 2 oz smoked bacon
- 1 cup heavy cream
- 3 lb pumpkin
- ¾-lb carrots
- 2 onions
- 2 oz butter
- 8 cups water
- 1 teaspoon curry powder
- ½ fresh truffle
- Salt, pepper

PREPARATION TIME
45 minutes

COOKING TIME
1 hour

Pumpkin Soup and Whipped Cream with Smoked Bacon and Fresh Truffle

Soften the gelatin in a bowl of cold water.

Cut the bacon in small pieces, brown in an ungreased frying pan. When golden, add the heavy cream and simmer for 3 minutes. Remove from heat, beat in the soaked gelatin and steep for 30 minutes. Strain the cream, pour into a whipped-cream dispenser, and set aside in the refrigerator.

Peel and chop the pumpkin, carrots, and onions. Melt the butter in a large pot. When the butter foams, add the chopped onions and the curry powder. Brown over a high heat for 10 minutes, stirring constantly. Add the chopped carrots and pumpkin, cover with 8 cups water, season to taste, and simmer for 1 hour, stirring occasionally.

When the vegetables are cooked, transfer to a food processor, add the cooking liquid, blend, and strain. Correct the seasoning and serve very hot, garnished with a mound of the bacon cream and a sliver of fresh truffle.

SERVES 4
- 2 Victoria pineapples
- ⅓ cup chilled heavy cream
- 2 tablespoons confectioners' sugar

For the passion-fruit crisps
- 1 lb passion fruit
- 5 tablespoons softened butter
- 5 tablespoons flour
- 1 cup confectioners' sugar
- 1 cup shredded almonds

For the vanilla butter
- ½ cup pineapple juice
- ½ cup sugar
- 3 tablespoons butter
- 2 vanilla pods

PREPARATION TIME
35 minutes

COOKING TIME
25 minutes

Pineapple Sautéed in Vanilla Butter with Passion-Fruit Crisps

Preheat the oven to 350°F (175°C).

• *Preparing the passion-fruit crisps*: Peel and cube the passion fruit. In a large bowl, mix together the butter, flour, confectioners' sugar, almonds, and cubed passion fruit. Use a teaspoon to form large rounds (about 1/5-inch [½ cm] thick and 3 inches [8 cm] in diameter) of this mixture on a greased baking sheet. Bake for 5 minutes. When crisp and golden, remove from oven and cool.

Cut the pineapples in half lengthwise, retaining the leaves. Cut out the flesh, remove the tough ribs, and slice into large cubes.

Boil the pineapple juice with the sugar until the mixture forms a syrup. Add the butter. Split the vanilla beans and scrape the seeds into the syrup. Boil for 2 more minutes and chill.

Whip the cream, add the confectioners' sugar, chill.

At serving time, sauté the cubed pineapple in the vanilla butter and serve warm in the pineapple shells, topped with the whipped cream and garnished with the passion fruit crisps.

SERVES 4
- 1 lb "Mara des Bois" strawberries
- ½ lb redcurrants
- 1 lb raspberries
- Dash of fresh lime juice

For the red wine syrup
- 4 cups red wine
- 1½ cups sugar
- 2 Chinese star anise
- 3 green cardamom seeds
- 4 peppercorns
- 1 stick cinnamon
- 1 vanilla pod
- 1 bunch fresh mint

PREPARATION TIME
30 minutes

COOKING TIME
1 hour

Fruit Soup with Red Wine Syrup

• *The night before*: Mix the red wine with the sugar and spices. Add the split and scraped vanilla pod with its seeds.

Simmer this mixture for 1 hour, to produce a light syrup. Remove from heat. Add the entire bunch of mint, including stems, to the hot syrup.

Cover with plastic film and steep overnight in the refrigerator.

• *Ten minutes before serving*: Stem and rinse the strawberries, carefully rinse the raspberries, stem and rinse the redcurrants.

Combine the fruit in a bowl and scoop equal portions onto serving plates. Sprinkle with a dash of lime juice.

Pour a little of the chilled wine syrup over the fruit and chill until ready to serve.

Menu of Dishes

APPETIZERS/STARTERS

·Beef Ravioli with a Vegetable Broth *Marc Meneau*	129
·Celery Cream with Horseradish, Large Brittany Oysters, Cucumber Aspic, Fresh Watercress, and Tarama *Nicolas Le Bec*	110
·Clams Baked in Embers with Smoked Olive Oil *Marc Meneau*	126
·Corsican Sea Urchins with Fennel Aspic *Georges Billon*	18
·Creamed Watercress with Sea Scallops *Arnaud Daguin*	72
·Cream of Prawn Soup *Arnaud Daguin*	72
·Eggs en Cocotte with Shrimps *Pierrot*	192
·Frogs'-Legs Tempura *Paul Bocuse*	34
·Goose Liver Terrine with Truffles *Marc Haeberlin*	94
·Green Salad Tartlets *Alain Passard*	144
·Hot-and-Cold Eggs with Chives *Alain Passard*	142
·Marinated Cuttlefish with Crisp Vegetables *Anne-Sophie Pic*	178
·Marinated Mackerel as Served at Café Epicerie *Nicolas Le Bec*	108
·Maroilles Cheese Pie *Pierrot*	192
·Mousseline of Red Peppers, Puréed Herbs, and Deep-Fried Prawns in an Orange-Flavored Crust *Gérard Boyer*	55
·An Ocean Medley of Sea-Anemone Fritters and Tender "Szechuan" Shellfish *Gérald Passédat*	160
·Oysters with Herb Butter *Michel Portos*	208
·Poached Duck Foie Gras with Tender Young Spinach *Arnaud Daguin*	77
·Poached Egg in Pancake Pockets on a Tartare of Marinated Fresh and Smoked Salmon with Herring Roe *Marc Haeberlin*	90
·Prawn Nems *Paul Bocuse*	36
·Pumpkin Soup and Whipped Cream with Smoked Bacon and Fresh Truffle *Mathieu Viannay*	248
·Raw Tuna Sashimi *Paul Bocuse*	34
·Rock Sea Urchins in the Shell with Granny-Smith Apple Cream *Anne-Sophie Pic*	181
·Sardines in Pastry *Mathieu Viannay*	244
· Scallop Canapés with Marrow *Marc Meneau*	130
·Trio of Spiced Prawns with Goats'-Cheese Tacos *Gérard Boyer*	52
·Truffle in Pastry "André Pic" *Anne-Sophie Pic*	176
·Zucchini Fritters *Gérard Boyer*	55

MAIN DISHES/ENTRÉES

· Beechwood-Smoked Potatoes *Alain Passard*	144
· Braised Pigs' Feet Stuffed with Foie Gras on a Bed of Red Champagne Lentils and Truffle Vinaigrette *Gérard Boyer*	58
· Braised Shoulder of Veal with Fresh Truffle *Mathieu Viannay*	248
· Bresse "Chicken in Mourning" with Sauce Suprême *Paul Bocuse*	41
· Cabbage Stuffed with Spring Vegetables *Alain Passard*	147
· Celery Root and Steamed Brittany-Lobster Ravioli with Fresh Basil *Nicolas Le Bec*	112
· Char with Iranian Caviar, Mousseline of Potatoes with Hazelnut Oil *Marc Haeberlin*	94
· Classic French Fries with Sea Salt *Pierrot*	195
· Cod in Salt Crust *Marc Meneau*	126
· Curried Risotto with Prawns *Mathieu Viannay*	246

· Filled Zucchini Blossoms and Steamed Medallions of Turbot with Provençal Herb Sauce *Nicolas Le Bec*	115
· Fillets of Red Mullet with Potato Scales *Paul Bocuse*	38
· Japanese-Style Squab *Michel Portos*	208
· Lobster "Petit Pagaille" with Sherry and Lemon Zest *Olivier Roellinger*	226
· Marmite Touquetoise *Pierrot*	196
· Medallions of Gilt-Head Bream Garnished with Eggplant Preserve and Pâté *Gérald Passédat*	162
· Moules Marinière *Pierrot*	195
· Oriental Mullet and Oyster Consommé with Shellfish and a Pistachio Topping *Gérald Passédat*	165
· Paul Haeberlin's Mousseline of Frogs' Legs *Marc Haeberlin*	93
· Red Mullet Stuffed with Brocciù *Georges Billon*	20
· Roast Stuffed Partridge and Myrtle with Chestnut Polenta *Georges Billon*	23
· Sautéed Meagre Fillets with Artichokes in Olive Oil *Arnaud Daguin*	78
· Sautéed Sliced Veal Kidneys, Quick-Cooked Spinach, Foie-Gras Flan, and Pan Gravy with Sherry *Gérard Boyer*	61
· Scallops with Oriental Spices *Olivier Roellinger*	228
· Spaghetti with Rock Lobster *Georges Billon*	20
· Turnips with Spiced Caramel *Anne-Sophie Pic*	176

DESSERTS

· Barley Sugar with Fruit Purée *Gérald Passédat*	166
· Brown-Sugar Pie *Pierrot*	198
· Candied Vanilla Mango, Sugar Crisps with Lemon Cream and Vanilla Ice Cream or Mango Sorbet *Anne-Sophie Pic*	182
· Crème Brûlée with Black Truffles and Warm, Tender Chocolate Cake served with Port-Wine Sauce and Chocolate Sorbet *Gérard Boyer*	62
· Fresh Sliced Mango and Pink-Grapefruit Segments Glazed with a Sauce of Verbena and Passion Fruit *Nicolas Le Bec*	116
· Fruit Soup with Red Wine Syrup *Mathieu Viannay*	250
· Glazed Rose Petals to Accompany a Glass of Gewürztraminer *Marc Haeberlin*	98
· Gugelhopf *Marc Haeberlin*	96
· Kouign Amann *Olivier Roellinger*	231
· An Invitation to Exotic Lands: Pineapple Millefeuille, with Rim and cider Grog *Olivier Roellinger*	234
· Peaches Haeberlin *Marc Haeberlin*	98
· Peaches in Caramelized Pastry *Arnaud Daguin*	80
· Peppery Spiced Strawberries *Marc Meneau*	132
· Pineapple Carpaccio with Candied Lime Peel *Paul Bocuse*	42
· Pineapple in Salt Crust *Alain Passard*	150
· Pineapple Sautéed in Vanilla Butter with Passion-Fruit Crisps *Mathieu Viannay*	250
· Pistachio Macaroons *Michel Portos*	214
· Tangerine Soufflé *Michel Portos*	214
· Tender Chestnut Cake *Georges Billon*	24
· Three Reasons to Love Figs *Michel Portos*	212
· Twelve-Spice Tomato Conserve *Alain Passard*	150

Addresses

GEORGES BILLON
Grand Hôtel Cala Rossa
Cala-Rossa 20137 Lecci
Tel: +33 (0)4 95 71 61 51
Fax: +33 (0)4 95 71 60 11
His suppliers
Cheese:
Les fromageries de Bala
Antoine Foata
20137 Porto-Vecchio
Olive oil:
Anne Amalric
Domaine de Marquiliani
20270 Aghione
Tel: +33 (0)4 95 56 64 02
Corsican and Sardinian fruit
and vegetables:
ETS Angelini
20137 Porto-Vecchio
Tel: +33 (0)4 95 70 19 13
Corsican veal:
Boucherie Cucchi
20137 Porto-Vecchio
Tel: +33 (0)4 95 70 38 00
Corsican fish and seafood:
Corse Marée
20200 Bastia
Tel: +33 (0)4 95 30 30 06
Poultry, strawberries and salads:
Ferme d'Azetta
20137 Muratello
Tel: +33 (0)4 95 70 02 32
Chestnut honey:
Michel Gacon
Tel: +33 (0)4 95 60 18 13
Fish and bouillabaisse:
André Fabi
Saint-Dominique
20137 Précoja

PAUL BOCUSE
L'Auberge du Pont de Collonges
40, quai de la Plage
69660 Collonges-au-Mont-d'Or
Tel: +33 (0)4 72 42 90 90
Fax: +33 (0)4 72 27 85 87
www.bocuse.fr
Brasseries Groupe Paul Bocuse
14, place Jules-Ferry
69006 Lyon
Tel: +33 (0)4 37 24 25 26
Rôtisserie Le Nord
18, rue Neuve
69002 Lyon
Tel: +33 (0)4 72 10 69 69
Fax: +33 (0)4 72 10 69 68
Restaurant Le Sud
11, place Antonin-Poncet
69002 Lyon
Tel: +33 (0)4 72 77 80 00
Fax: +33 (0)4 72 77 80 01
Restaurant L'Est
Gare des Brotteaux
69006 Lyon
Tel: +33 (0)4 37 24 25 26
Fax: +33 (0)4 37 24 25 25

Brasserie L'Ouest
1, quai du Commerce
69009 Lyon
Tel: +33 (0)4 37 64 64 64
Fax: +33 (0)4 37 64 64 65
His suppliers
Chocolate:
Bernachon
42, cour Franklin-Roosevelt
69006 Lyon
Tel: +33 (0)4 78 24 37 98
Fax: +33 (0)4 78 52 67 77
Fish:
Pupier
Halles de Lyon
102, cours Lafayette
69003 Lyon
Tel: +33 (0)4 78 62 37 26
Fax: +33 (0)4 78 60 45 54
Cheese:
Renée Richard
Halles de Lyon
102, cours Lafayette
69003 Lyon
Tel: +33 (0)4 78 62 30 78
Fax: +33 (0)4 78 71 75 09

GÉRARD BOYER
Boyer "Les Crayères "
64, boulevard Henry-Vasnier
51100 Reims
Tel: +33 (0)3 26 82 80 80
Fax: +33 (0)3 26 82 65 52
www.gerardboyer.com
His suppliers
Cheese:
Daniel Boujon
74200 Thonon-les-Bains
Tel: +33 (0)4 50 71 07 68
Lautrec rose garlic:
Jacqueline Barthe
81440 Lautrec
Tel: +33 (0)5 63 74 30 68
Gray shallots:
Jean-Marie Caillot
51320 Coole
Tel: +33 (0)3 26 74 32 23
Sheep's-milk yogurt:
François Laluc
51800 Villers-en-Argonne
Tel: +33 (0)3 26 60 84 93
Bussy turnips, dwarf pumpkins,
Hubbard squash:
Jean-Luc Galichet
51600 Bussy-le-Château
Tel: +33 (0)3 26 67 56 80

ARNAUD DAGUIN
Les Platanes
32, avenue Beau-Soleil
64200 Biarritz
Tél. : +33 (0)5 59 23 13 68
His suppliers
Duck foie gras:
Maisons Lafitte conserveries
455, route Béarn

40500 Montaut
Tel: +33 (0)5 58 76 40 40
Biarritz market,
all morning, every day:
Fruit and vegetables:
Véronique Marmazinsky
Poultry and lamb:
Peyo Telleria
Ham:
André Hargous
Cheese:
· Mille et un fromages
· Madame Olga
· Aupetit (in particular
for goats' cheese)
Fish and cooked dishes:
Robert Aragües
Wines from the South-west
and from Languedoc:
Le Cellier des Halles
Christian Bedat
8, rue des Halles
64200 Biarritz
Tel: +33 (0)5 59 24 21 64
Fax: +33 (0)5 59 22 36 14

MARC HAEBERLIN
Auberge de l'Ill
68970 Illhaeusern
Tel: +33 (0)3 89 71 89 00
Fax: +33 (0)3 89 71 82 83
His suppliers
Lamb:
L'Allaiton d'Aveyron
Monsieur Greffeuille
Le Bayle
12390 Rignac
Tel: +33 (0)5 65 80 82 24
Fax: +33 (0)5 65 80 88 00
Fish:
· Rungiest
55, rue Marché Gare
67200 Strasbourg
Tel: +33 (0)3 88 28 47 28
Fax: +33 (0)3 88 26 32 48
· SDAB
Vallon Saint-Guenolé BP 31
29660 Carantec
Tel: +33 (0)2 98 67 00 46
Fax: +33 (0)2 98 78 30 75
Meat:
NBA Boucherie Nivernaises
99, rue du Faubourg-Saint-Honoré
Tel: +33 (0)1 43 59 11 02
Fax: +33 (0)1 42 25 12 32
Wine:
· Hugel
3, rue 1er-Armée-Française
68340 Riquewihr
Tel: +33 (0)3 89 47 92 15
Fax: +33 (0)3 89 49 00 10
· Beyer
2, rue 1re-Armée
68420 Eguisheim
Tel: +33 (0)3 89 21 62 30
Fax: +33 (0)3 89 23 93 63

· Trimbach
15, route Bergheim
68150 Ribeauville
Tel: +33 (0)3 89 73 60 30
Fax: +33 (0)3 89 73 89 04

NICOLAS LE BEC
Les Loges
6, rue Bœuf
69005 Lyon
Tel: +33 (0)4 72 77 44 40
Fax: +33 (0)4 72 41 88 17
www.courdesloges.com
Épicerie les Loges
6, rue Bœuf
69005 Lyon
Tel: +33 (0)4 72 77 44 40
Fax: +33 (0)4 72 41 88 17
His suppliers
Speciality butcher:
Metzger
Olivier Metzger
45, rue du Poitou
Bâtiment D8 PLA 440
94619 Rungis Cedex
Tel: +33 (0)1 41 80 10 30
Fax: +33 (0)1 46 75 97 96
Cold meats:
Sibilia
Colette Sibilia
Halles de Lyon
102, cours Lafayette
69003 Lyon
Tel: +33 (0)4 78 62 36 28
Fax: +33 (0)4 78 60 86 07
Foie gras:
Masse
Frédéric Masse
Bâtiment 1
34, rue Casimir-Périer
69297 Lyon Cedex
Tel: +33 (0)4 78 42 65 29
Fax: +33 (0)4 72 41 02 06
Mediterranean fish:
Cervera Marée
Jérôme Cervera
ZI de La Frayère
06150 Cannes La Bocca
Tel: +33 (0)4 93 47 02 03
Fax: +33 (0)4 93 47 83 90
Atlantic fish:
Le Corsaire
Mareyeur de Saint-Malo
Bâtiment A
Terre-plein des Servannais
35400 Saint-Malo
Tel: +33 (0)2 99 82 82 42
Fax: +33 (0)2 99 81 45 14
Produce from Les Landes,
International fine foods:
Corest
Monsieur Dariel
77, rue de Casablanca
40230 Saint-Vincent-de-Tyrosse
Tel: +33 (0)5 58 77 24 15
Fax: +33 (0)5 58 77 24 10

Cheese:
· Boujon
Daniel Boujon
7, rue Saint-Sébastien
74200 Thonon-les-Bains
Tel: +33 (0)4 50 71 07 68
Fax: +33 (0)4 50 81 90 88
· Renée Richard
Halles de Lyon
102, cours Lafayette
69003 Lyon
Tel: +33 (0)4 78 62 30 78
Fax: +33 (0)4 78 71 75 09
Rhône valley wine:
Georges Vernay
1, rue Nationale
69420 Condrieu
Tel: +33 (0)4 74 56 81 81
Fax: +33 (0)4 74 56 60 98
Mâcon wines:
Merlin
Olivier Merlin
71960 La Roche-Vineuse
Tel: +33 (0)3 85 36 62 09
Fax: +33 (0)3 85 36 66 45

MARC MENEAU
L'Espérance
89450 Saint-Père-sous-Vézelay
Tel: + 33 (0)3 86 33 39 10
Fax: +33 (0)3 86 33 26 15
www.marc-meneau-esperance.com
His suppliers
Fruit and vegetables:
Ets Gourlet
Rond-point de la Croix Verte
89200 Avallon
Tel: +33 (0)3 86 34 14 87
Fax: +33 (0)3 86 34 57 77
Meat:
Ets Jean Denaux
Rue de l'Industrie
89100 Malay-le-Grand
Tel: +33 (0)3 86 97 28 00
Fax: +33 (0)3 86 97 26 44
Fish:
Art'Viv
Les pêcheurs artisans
Les viviers-Beg
AR Vilin
22820 Plougrescant
Tel: +33 (0)2 96 92 51 30
Poultry:
Miéral
25, route de Châlon
01340 Montrevel-en-Bresse
Tel: +33 (0)4 74 30 81 13
Fax: +33 (0)4 74 30 88 75

ALAIN PASSARD
L'Arpège
84, rue Varenne
75007 Paris
Tel: +33 (0)1 47 05 09 06
Fax: +33 (0)1 44 18 98 39
www.alain-passard.com

His suppliers
Butter:
Jean-Yves Bordier
19, rue Claude-Bernard
35400 Saint-Malo
Tel: +33 (0)2 99 81 55 50
Cheese:
Bernard Antony
5, rue de la Montagne
68480 Vieux-Ferrette
Tel: +33 (0)3 89 40 42 22

GÉRALD PASSÉDAT
Le Petit Nice-Passédat
Anse de Maldormé
Corniche J.-F. Kennedy
13007 Marseilles
Tel: +33 (0)4 91 59 25 92
Fax: +33 (0)4 91 59 28 08
www.petitnice-passedat.com
His suppliers
Cheese:
Hervé Mons
Le Pré Normand
42370 Saint-Haon-le-Chatel
Tel: +33 (0)4 77 64 40 79
Fax: +33 (0)4 77 64 44 18
Fruit, vegetables and wild mushrooms:
Gourmand de Nature
Marc Lopez
3, place des Bergers
13630 Eyragues
Tel/Fax: +33 (0)4 90 24 90 12
Olive oil:
Yacinthe Bellon
Moulin à huile de Bédarrides
13990 Fontvielle
Tel: +33 (0)4 90 54 70 04
Fax: +33 (0)4 90 54 78 99
Chocolate:
Pralus
8, rue Charles-de-Gaulle
42300 Roanne
Tel: +33 (0)4 77 71 24 10
Fax: +33 (0)4 77 70 30 63

ANNE-SOPHIE PIC
Pic
285, avenue Victor-Hugo
26000 Valence
Tel: +33 (0)4 75 44 15 32
Fax: +33 (0)4 75 40 96 03
www.pic-valence.com
Her suppliers
Salad:
Fleur Délice
Jean-Luc Raillon
Saint-Vincent-de-la-Commanderie
Fish:
Cervera
40, avenue Michel-Jourdan
06150 Cannes La Bocca
Tel: +33 (0)4 93 47 02 03
5, allée Gabians
06150 Cannes La Bocca
Tel: +33 (0)4 93 47 83 90

Wine:
· Jaboulet
Route de Valence
26600 La Roche-de-Glun
Tel: +33 (0)4 75 84 68 93
Fax: +33 (0)4 75 84 56 14
· Michel Chapoutier
Châteaux des Estubiers
26290 Les Granges-Gontardes
Tel: +33 (0)4 75 98 54 78
Fax: +33 (0)4 75 98 54 81
· Jean-Louis Chaves
Rue Mûres
07300 Mauves
Tel: +33 (0)4 75 07 91 97
Fax: +33 (0)4 75 07 91 98

PIERROT
Le Bistrot de Pierrot
6, place de Béthune
59800 Lille
Tel: +33 (0)3 20 57 14 09
Fax: +33 (0)3 20 30 93 13
www.pierrot-de-lille.com
His suppliers
Chicory:
Daniel Chauwin
28, rue de Cambrai
62860 Épinoy
Tel: +33 (0)3 21 59 57 74
Potatoes:
Monsieur Taffin
178, ZI du Moulin
BP 18
59193 Erquinghem-Lys
Tel: +33 (0)3 28 82 08 20
Pastries:
Meert Traditions
27, rue Esquermoise
59000 Lille
Tel: +33 (0)3 20 57 07 44
Beer:
La Cave des Flandres
Béatrice, Pierrot's fiancée
20, rue de l'Église
59190 Hazebrouck
Tel: +33 (0)3 28 41 65 26

MICHEL PORTOS
Le Saint James
3, place Camille-Hosteins
33270 Bouliac
Tel: +33 (0)5 57 97 06 00
Fax: +33 (0)5 56 20 92 58
His suppliers
Poultry:
Bertrand Hazéra
Élevage des Barthes
48, route de Créon
33750 Camarsac.
Lamb:
L'allaiton d'Aveyron
Monsieur Greffeuille,
Le Bayle
12390 Rignac
Tel: +33 (0)5 65 80 82 24

Oils:
Jean-Marc Montegottero
29, rue des Écharmeaux
69430 Beaujeu
Tel: +33 (0)4 74 69 28 06
Fax: +33 (0)4 74 04 87 09
Cheese:
Hervé Mons
(Meilleur Ouvrier de France)
Le Pré Normand
42370 Saint-Haon-Le-Chatel
Tel: +33 (0)4 77 64 40 79
Fax: +33 (0)4 77 64 44 18
Specialty produce:
Le Potager de la Citadelle
Anne-Sophie Loubière
33190 Fontet
Tel: +33 (0)5 56 61 14 37

OLIVIER ROELLINGER
Les Maisons de Bricourt
1, rue Duguesclin
35260 Cancale
Tel: +33 (0)2 99 89 64 76
Fax: +33 (0)2 99 89 88 47
www.maisons-de-bricourt.com
His suppliers
Cold meats:
Jean Lepage
Saint-Servan market on
Tuesday and Friday,
Paramé on Wednesday,
Dinard on Saturday.
Tel: +33 (0)2 99 56 00 38
Butter:
Jean-Yves Bordier,
9, rue de l'Orme
35400 Saint-Malo
Tel: +33 (0)2 99 40 88 79
Fax: +33 (0)2 99 56 09 41
Market gardeners:
La famille Robin
Marché de Saint-Servan
et de Paramé
Tel: +33 (0)2 99 81 65 80
Oysters:
Michel Daniel
Chez Mazo
37, quai Kennedy
35260 Cancale
Tel: +33 (0)2 99 89 62 66
Fax: +33 (0)2 99 89 90 88
Les Lices market:
Rennes, every Saturday
morning, local women
selling herbs, roses,
and vegetables.
Yves Bocel and his sons
for slender leeks, sand-
grown carrots.
Annie Bertin for her
herbs and aromatic plants.
Cancale fisheries:
Le Vauhariot
35260 Cancale
Tel: +33 (0)2 99 89 69 34

Addresses
(continued)

MATHIEU VIANNAY
Mathieu Viannay
47, avenue Foch
69006 Lyon
Tel: +33 (0)4 78 89 55 19
Fax: +33 (0)4 78 89 08 39
His suppliers
Cold meats:
Sibilia
Colette Sibilia
Halles de Lyon
102, cours Lafayette
69003 Lyon
Tel: +33 (0)4 78 62 36 28
Fax: +33 (0)4 78 60 86 07
Cheese:
Madame Renée Richard
Halles de Lyon
102, cours Lafayette
69003 Lyon
Tel: +33 (0)4 78 62 30 78
Fax: +33 (0)4 78 71 75 09
Goat's cheese:
Les chèvres de la ferme du Puy
07240 Saint-Jean-Chambre
Tel: +33 (0)4 75 58 14 55
Fish:
SDAB
Vallon Saint-Guenolé BP 31
29660 Carantec
Tel: +33 (0)2 98 67 00 46
Fax: +33 (0)2 98 78 30 75
Vegetables:
Monsieur Cottendin
MIN
34, rue Casimir-Périer
69002 Lyon
Tel: +33 (0)4 72 41 02 03
Fax: +33 (0)4 72 41 05 79
Meat:
Boucherie GBM
44, route du Mans
69100 Villeurbanne
Tel: +33 (0)4 72 04 11 00
Fax: +33 (0)4 72 04 14 40
Farmed pork:
Henri Peziat "Gorré"
29780 Plouhinec
Tel: +33 (0)2 98 91 32 60
Snails:
L'Escargot de Monsieur Chauvin
380, route des Fermes
"Chânes"
01360 La Valbonne
Tel: +33 (0)4 78 06 07 49

Bibliography

PAUL BOCUSE
· Bocuse, Paul. *Les Meilleures Recettes des régions de France.* Paris: Éditions Flammarion, 2002.
· Bocuse, Paul. *Bocuse's regional french cooking.* Paris: Éditions Flammarion, 2002.
· Bocuse, Paul. *La Cuisine du gibier.* Paris: Éditions Flammarion, 2000.
· Bocuse, Paul. *Bocuse à la carte: menus pourla table familiale.* Paris: Éditions Flammarion, 1999.
· Bocuse, Paul. *La Cuisine du marché.* Paris: Éditions Flammarion, 1998.
· Bocuse, Paul. *Cuisine des régions de France.* Paris: Éditions Flammarion, 1997.
· Bocuse, Paul. *Bocuse dans votre cuisine: 222 recettes.* Paris: Éditions Flammarion, 1997.
· Bocuse, Paul. *La Bonne Chère.* Paris: Éditions Flammarion, 1995.
· Bocuse, Paul. *Paul Bocuse's Regional French Cooking.* Paris: Éditions Flammarion, 1991.
· Bocuse, Paul. *Cuisine de France.* Paris: Éditions Flammarion, 1990.
· Bocuse, Paul. *Bon Appétit.* Paris: Éditions Flammarion, 1989.
· Bocuse, Paul. *Bocuse à la Carte.* New York: Pantheon Books, 1987.
· Bocuse, Paul. *Viandes et Poissons.* Paris: Éditions Flammarion, 1984.
· Bocuse, Paul. *Potages et Entrées.* Paris: Éditions Flammarion, 1984.
· Bocuse, Paul. *Paul Bocuse in your Kitchen.* New York: Pantheon Books, 1982.
· Bocuse, Paul. *La Cuisine du marché.* Paris: Éditions Flammarion, 1980.
· Bocuse, Paul. *Paul Bocuse's French Cooking.* New York: Pantheon Books, 1977.

GÉRARD BOYER
· Lefebvre, Caroline. *Le Vinaigre dévoilé.* Geneva: Édition Aubanel, 2000.

MARC HAEBERLIN
· Haeberlin, Paul, Jean-Pierre Haeberlin, and Marc Haeberlin. *Les Recettes de l'Auberge de l'Ill.*
  Paris: Éditions Flammarion, 1982.
· Haeberlin, Marc. *L'Alsace gourmande de Marc Haeberlin.* Paris: Éditions Albin Michel, 1995.
· Morgenthaler, Simone and Jean-Pierre Haeberlin. *Le Long de l'Ill.*
  Strasbourg: Éditions La Nuée bleue, 2002.

MARC MENEAU
· Meneau, Marc and Annie Caen. *Les salades: du potager à l'assiette.* Geneva: Éditions Minerva, 2001.
· Meneau, Marc and Annie Caen. *La cuisine des monastères.* Paris: Éditions La Martinière, 1999.
· Meneau, Marc and Annie Caen. *Musée gourmand.* Paris: Éditions Le Chêne, 1992.
· Meneau, Marc. *La cuisine en fêtes.* Paris: Éditions Robert Laffont, 1986.

ANNE-SOPHIE PIC
· Pic, Anne-Sophie. *L'artichaut : dix façons de le préparer.* Paris: Éditions de l'Épure, 2002.

PIERROT
· Coucke, Pierre. *Goûtez-moi ça… les recettes de Pierrot.* Lille, Éditions La Voix du Nord, 1997.
· Coucke, Pierre. *Goûtez-moi ça… aux fourneaux avec Pierrot.* Paris: Éditions L'Oeil d'Or, 1999.
· Coucke, Pierre. *Goûtez-moi ça… les nouvelles recettes de Pierrot.* Lille, Éditions La Voix du Nord, 2001.
· Coucke, Pierre. *Aimer la cuisine du Nord-Pas-de-Calais et de la Picardie.*
  Rennes: Éditions Ouest-France, 2002.
· Coucke, Pierre. *Cuisine du Nord-Pas-de-Calais et de la Picardie d'hier et d'aujourd'hui.*
  Rennes: Éditions Ouest-France, 2002.

OLIVIER ROELLINGER
· Roellinger, Olivier. *Le Livre d'Olivier Roellinger.* Avec la collaboration de Daniel Crozes,
  Colette Gouvion, Christian Millau. Rodez: Éditions du Rouergue, 1994.
· Roellinger, Olivier. *Couleurs de Bretagne.* Paris: Éditions Flammarion, 1999.

Greateful thanks: Philippe Martin from the Studio Mallet-Martin at Lyon. Serge and Mina Malvoisin's bakery at Lens. Jean-Luc Lescaillet-Taffin, grower of patatoes at Erquinghem-Lys.